Finding Joy For The Suicidal
A Mother's Account of her Autistic Child's Crisis
By: Cyndi C.

Editing by:
Joey V.
&
Michael V.

Published by

Copyright @ 2021 by Calm The Qualm, llc. All Rights Reserved. This publication may not be reproduced in whole or in part by any means without written permission from the publisher, except for the purpose of quoting brief passages either for the purpose of reviewing this book, or with proper attribution.

The Publisher may be contacted in writing at:
Calm The Qualm
P. O. Box 170, Clarklake, MI, 49234

Proper attribution must include both the author of the passage and "Finding Joy For The Suicidal" in a way that clearly marks the origin of the passage.

ISBN: 978-1-7373754-0-1 (Hard Cover)   First Printing, 2021
ISBN: 978-1-7373754-1-8 (Paperback)   First Printing, 2021
ISBN: 978-1-7373754-2-5 (Ebook)   First Printing, 2021

Cover Design & Formatting by Joey V.
Cover Photo by Cyndi C.
Three Sons Photo by Renee Janofski
Everything Flag Photo by James Haldane

Scripture taken from The Modern English Version. Copyright @ 2014 by Military Bible Association. Used by Permission. All rights reserved.

Finding Joy For The Suicidal
A Mother's Account of her Autistic Child's Crisis

By: Cyndi C.

Notice of Factual Basis:

These are actual incidents, but the names and locations have been changed to protect the identities and confidentiality of the parties involved.

Table of Contents

Foreword: How to Save a Life

    Page 1

Our Story

    Page 7

    Chapter 1: Why This Book Exists

    Page 8

    Chapter 2: Ready or Not, Here We Go!

    Page 13

    Chapter 3: What went Wrong

    Page 19

    Chapter 4: The Wyoming Years

    Page 27

    Chapter 5: Starting Over Again

    Page 33

    Chapter 6: Miscommunication Based Bad Behavior

    Page 37

    Chapter 7: Autism Apparent

    Page 41

    Chapter 8: Unstable Living

    Page 45

    Chapter 9: The Difference Between a Need and a Want

    Page 49

    Chapter 10: Losing Control

    Page 53

    Chapter 11: The Difference a Friend Can Make

    Page 57

    Chapter 12: Dating in Secret

    Page 62

    Chapter 13: A Pity Party is a Lame Party

    Page 67

Chapter 14: Vocalizing Fears
                                                Page 71

Chapter 15: Happy Memories
                                                Page 74

Chapter 16: Autism for Two
                                                Page 77

Chapter 17: Medications List Side Effects For a Reason
                                                Page 80

Chapter 18: Getting Through Middle School
                                                Page 82

Chapter 19: The Pool and the Beanbag Chair
                                                Page 86

Chapter 20: A More Proactive Approach
                                                Page 90

Chapter 21: Where are we now?
                                                Page 94

Lessons Learned
                                                Page 98

Chapter 22: A Willingness to Listen is Powerful
                                                Page 99

Chapter 23: Avoid Tunnel Vision & Assess Your Options
                                                Page 102

Chapter 24: Reaching for the Lifeline
                                                Page 105

Chapter 25: On Parenting
                                                Page 112

Chapter 26: Letting Go of Best Laid Plans
                                                Page 119

Chapter 27: Keep Going
                                                Page 126

Special Thanks
                                                Page 129

About the Author
                                                Page 130

Foreword: How to Save a Life

By: Joey V.

If you picked up this book because you know someone who is suicidal and are looking for advice, this chapter is for you. My name is Joey, and I have been there. Not looking for advice, I mean the pit of despair that makes you contemplate death as a possible alternative to living. I have a different and more personal perspective on the topic than any psychologist is likely to be able to give you, and I have written this first chapter at my Mom's request to hopefully give you and the person you are trying to save, the hope and practical advice you need to keep going and find happiness.

Let's start with some good news:

1. There is not a man who is living who truly wants to die.
2. If someone tells you they are suicidal, then you are in a very privileged position. They obviously love and trust you greatly. People don't announce their weakness to strangers or enemies, and suicidal contemplation comes from a feeling of powerlessness that you can't escape, so you can be sure that you are important to them if they are willing to open up to you.
3. They also have not decided that they truly want to die. Nothing can save the man who has forsaken the will to live. Such a man will depart swiftly without reaching out for others to pull them back.
4. Even people who have made suicide attempts don't truly want to die. I personally can vouch for this. As someone who in middle school strangled myself three times, smothered myself with a pillow half a dozen times, threatened to stab myself so often that my mom threw away every steak knife in the house, and reached to grab the wheel of the car to swerve it into oncoming traffic. These are some extreme actions for someone who was only 12-14 at the time, but if you really think about it none of them are particularly likely to succeed if you don't want them to.

Suicide attempts that "fail" are not failures they are painstakingly crafted cries for help that beg others to take notice because actions speak louder than words, and the suicidal person is at the end of their rope and they have run out of options that they feel will be effective and are desperately hoping for something to change in response. My advice to you, as someone who cares for them is to listen and take action. Make the changes that they need.

My advice to them, as someone with experience attempting suicide, is cutting is never the answer. It has no more impact than any other form of suicide attempt, but it is very painful, makes a bio-hazardous mess that can make others sick, and can cause undesirable side-effects such as circulatory issues or infection. Even if you plan to actually die this time, cutting still isn't the answer because it is sooo slow. Bleeding out is boring and takes way longer than you would think.

What? Were you expecting me to advise they not make suicide attempts? If their problems could be solved by some stranger writing a book telling them to straighten themselves out, they wouldn't be contemplating suicide in the first place. I don't know them or what they are going through, but I know their despair and I respect them for baring with it, even if they are attempting suicide. There are only two ways suicide attempts stop, either things get better, or the suicidal person gives up crying for help, and kills themselves proper and you take them off your contacts list. I'm not going to tell someone to stop calling for help if I'm not going to be there to support them.

That said, if you are suicidal, and your friends ignore your suicide confession, and/or attempts, all hope is not lost. That just means that either your friends are also going through tough times and simply feel they can't help you personally (perhaps because they don't know how), or you have terrible friends and you can go out and get some better ones. If you're not sure which it is, you can just ask them. Surprisingly, bad friends tend to be shockingly honest about it, because they don't care.

And now for a few reality checks:

1. In most cases, it is the suicidal person themselves that needs to change in order to find happiness. Think about it, there are people in ultra max-security prisons who live in concrete rooms that are shamefully small. They are never allowed out of solitary confinement, but they don't want to die. It isn't the circumstances that drag the soul of a man into the pit of despair, no we reach down into the abyss to grasp that which we have lost, but can not bare to let go. For me, the root of my problem was when I asked my Dad when he would move back in, and he told me, "Don't be a dumb-ass, don't you fucking get it? I'm done with you. I don't want a family anymore. I'm not coming back!" So my fear of abandonment if I couldn't live up to an undefined standard of expectations became the chains that wrapped me and dragged me down into the hell hole that would be my life for the next seven or so years.
2. On a similar note, you will not be able to empathize with the pain of a suicidal person. It is deeper than you could ever imagine. Unless you have been pushed that far yourself, you will never be able to fathom the depth of their despair, and their problems may even sound trivial to you, but know this, the pain is very real, and they are reaching out to you, because they can't see a way out on their own. You don't have to understand what they are going through, but accept it, and never deny it.

3. If someone tells you they are suicidal, they are reaching to you personally for help. They have told you their deepest secrets, If they wanted other people to know, they would have told them themselves. Don't immediately let the rest of the world know. Gossip is betrayal of that trust. Encourage them to open up and seek the help they need themselves, if you put them in a mental ward without their permission, they very well may hate you for it, which is a shame since they trusted you enough to reach out to you.
4. Honestly ask yourself, "How much does this person mean to me? What would I be willing to give up to keep them alive?" Talk and gifts are cheap. Time is the currency of love. If you are unwilling or unable to give them the support they need, advise them to seek help elsewhere, don't let them down by tossing them a rope, but then refusing to hold onto the other end!
5. Never threaten to kill yourself in response to someone else's suicide. Double suicides are considered romantic by some people, and they might take you up on it, after all, they were considering death anyway, why turn down an offer for a romantic tragic one?
6. Remember that even if they kill themselves, it isn't your fault. It was ultimately their choice to make, and no matter how hard you try, you can't save someone who doesn't want your help.

When I was a child in third grade, we had a pool in our backyard. My brother hated that pool, but I personally loved it and would swim in it every day I could, and would look out at it and sigh every day that it wasn't clean. One day I saw my brother climb into the pool and just lie face down in the water. Needless to say, I was out to the pool in no time, to ask what was up! My brother informed me that he hated the pool and planned to lay face down in the water until he passed out and drowned.

I replied with less than ideal speech craft, "I love you, and I love this pool. If you die in this pool, you are dead, and it's between you and God, but I will lose my best friend and my pool and there is no way in hell I'm going to let you take that away from me!" My selfish reasoning did not convince my brother not to drown himself in our pool, so I stood in the pool with him for hours pulling his head out of the water every time he tried until we were both badly sunburned. Where my words failed to reach him in his despair, my dedication could and he kept living and remains my greatest friend to this day.

Our Story

Since the next several chapters are going to primarily focus on what we went through to provide context for the lessons we've learned I'd like to take this moment to pray for you and your loved ones:

Our God and Father, Please bless the readers of this book and those they hold dear, be with them, and guide them in the right direction. Protect them from circumstances beyond their control, and give them opportunities to grow both as individuals and in their relationships with each other and you. Ease their burdens and grant them peace despite the difficulties they face. Help them find joy each day, and fill them with gratitude for all the blessings in their life. Thank you for your unending faithfulness, and the love and hope you ceaselessly give.
Amen.

A quick note before we start this journey down Memory Lane, I have to tell you, it's been years, over a decade in fact. Although I'm doing my best to tell you the truth about all we went through, it's merely the truth as I remember it. I was sleep deprived, over-worked and scared out of my mind. It is not the most objective viewpoint to look at this from. This is my story as I remember it. My sons, Michael & Joey may remember things differently, and perhaps only God knows the complete truth of the matter. Now, with that disclaimer out of the way, fill up your coffee cup, my friend, because it's about to get real!

Chapter 1

Why This Book Exists

When I was struggling, I wanted to hear from the Moms who'd traveled my path and their kids survived. No matter how hard I looked, all those voices were all strangely silent, which made me think our chances were doomed. The memories are so fresh in my mind, it could have been yesterday...

Splish, splash, splish. The wipers furiously pushed the pouring rain away as I waited in the drive up lane at the bank to cash my measly little check, barely enough to pay the rent.

"Please, no chit chat! I'm trying to keep my composure." I silently pleaded in my mind, as I put the check in the little tube. "Just cash, please." I said and was relieved when I got out of there with the cash in hand. "So far, so good." I thought to myself, as every alarm in my head fired off at once.

"The rent is due today!" My conscience warned. I pushed the thought out of mind as I circled around to find a parking spot in front of the bookstore With steeled resolve, I pushed through the doors and immediately started scouring the shelves for the book I wanted… no needed… no… couldn't live without. Money was no object. I'd already decided. I would get this book, no matter what! But where would it be? Psychology? Self-Help? Parenting? Christian Living? I frantically checked them all, and as I neared the end of the last shelf, the realization hit me like a ton of bricks! There was no such book. At least not here in the largest bookstore in one of the largest cities of our state.

I ran for the door trying hard to hold my composure, until I could get to my car. A sales clerk stopped me near the door and asked, "May I help you Ma'am?"

"No." I blurted, "I don't think anyone can." The floodgates burst in my eyes and embarrassing tears poured down my face as I pushed past him and ran for my car. I swung the door open to beautiful sunlight and gawking strangers wondering what was wrong with me as they headed into the store. "Where's that rain now, when I need it?" I thought to myself. "Can't anything go right today?"

In the safety of my car, all the memories of the night before came flooding back. The night before, my son had been carted away in a police vehicle for attempting suicide. They took him to Emergency Mental Health, and I followed along in my own vehicle. I waited helplessly in the waiting room while the Doctor talked with him behind locked doors. I wish I could say this was new to me, but it wasn't.

The truth was I'd called 911 on my son enough times it was beginning to be a ritual. The police knew us, and I'd long since quit caring what my neighbors thought of police cars with flashing lights in my driveway. Our lives were spiraling out of control, and I was desperate to find someone who could help me save my son. That's why I was so deflated when I saw him come out from behind those doors with the psychiatrist who said, "Okay, Mom, you can take him home. He promises not to kill himself tonight."

I had no choice but to take him home. Single Moms on tight budgets can't insist on extra therapies, counseling, medical tests, or anything else for that matter! But as I lay awake in bed, I couldn't help but wonder, "He said he won't kill himself tonight, but can we even trust his word on that? And say he doesn't kill himself tonight, what about tomorrow, next week, or next month? Can I ever afford to take my eyes off him long enough to sleep again?"

The only way I'd been able to get through the day at work was by promising myself I'd stop by the bookstore on the way home and get a book on helping your teenager overcome suicidal tendencies. But now I knew no such book existed, and I still needed to go home and face my son again. Now what?

"Please God," I silently prayed, "Get my baby through this and I'll reach back and write the book. That way the next Mom who comes here looking, will find it." With that promise made, I headed home to my troubled life...

Seven years later, I gushed to my sister, Tracey, over coffee, "I was so proud of him! To think all we went through together, and God saw us through it all. He even graduated with Honors! A promise is a promise. I guess I have a book to write!"

"You know you can never write that book, don't you?" Tracey asked.

"Why not? I promised God." I complained.

"Just because God saw you through, doesn't mean the same thing would work for someone else. Some teenagers really kill themselves, Cyndi. You can't promise their parents that they won't. That's why the book doesn't exist. You could be offering false hope. If their child dies, you might even be liable."

With those words of warning, I sipped my coffee and thought it over. When she's right, she's right, and I couldn't take the risk. But every time I thought of all God had done for us, and the promise I'd made, I couldn't help but regret that I'd failed to keep my end of the bargain.

Some time later, I found myself headed to minor surgery. They helped me onto the table, buckled me around the waist, and strapped my arms down as they prepared to sedate me. Because of my various allergies and asthma, the anesthesiologists acted a little nervous about the sedation process. The first anesthesiologist bowed out and a different one showed up to sedate me, so I was beginning to feel a little nervous too.

When they put the gas mask over my face, it occurred to me that there was no turning back now. I had relinquished the power of my life or death to the people in that room. I thought about all the things I'd planed to do, but didn't get done. I remembered my promise to write the book, and I regretted I hadn't finished it. When I woke from surgery, I had a new resolve to keep my promise and help those struggling Moms out there, but how? I still couldn't promise them anything. What they needed was hope they could count on!

If the book I'd hoped to find is impossible to write perhaps that just means I was looking for the wrong book. I may not have all the answers, but I do have experience, and I will share it with you along with what I learned in the hopes that it may help you as well.

That said I may have experienced something similar and am sharing my insights, but I'm by no means an expert. Think of this book less as an instruction manual and more as a lighthouse – a shining beacon that pierces the dark to help you find your own way to shore. Ultimately your choices and the consequences of them are between you and God, but fear not for even if you know not where to turn or how to navigate the rocky waters God will be with you, and with his guidance all things work together for good. If you let God work things out according to His timing and His plan, you might not find happiness, but you will find joy.

"The LORD is my shepherd; I shall not want.
He makes me lie down in green pastures; He leads me beside still waters. He restores my soul; He leads me in paths of righteousness for His name's sake. Even though I walk through the valley of the shadow of death, I will fear no evil; for You are with me; Your rod and Your staff, they comfort me."
- Psalm 23:1-4 MEV

"Trust in the Lord with all your heart and lean not on your own understanding; in all your ways submit to Him, and He will direct your paths."
- Proverbs 3:5-6 MEV

Chapter 2

Ready or Not, Here We Go!

When my first son Michael was born, I was so ready to have a child! It had been three long years of holidays with no child around to spoil. Despite our best efforts, I hadn't gotten pregnant. I had everyone in our prayer group praying we could have a child, and finally that prayer was answered. As I held my baby in that hospital room, it suddenly dawned on me how ill-prepared I was to be a mother. "Are they crazy?" I thought to myself. "Are they really going to let me walk out of here with this precious little guy? Don't they know I don't have a clue how to raise him? Poor little guy. I should at least have to pass a test or something!" I remember apologizing to Michael that he got stuck with me for a Mom. I promised him I'd do my best to keep him alive and well, and with that, and a few books I bought on the subject of raising a baby, I left the hospital to begin our new life.

Raising Michael started out being a breeze. Weighing 10lbs. 8oz. At birth, he quickly met all his bench marks. Within two weeks, he was sleeping through the night and holding his head up high. He was a sweet little guy, and very willing to please. He was great at playing independently, and wasn't afraid to play alone in his room while I cooked or cleaned in a different room. This parenting thing was a breeze! I was so excited to be pregnant again the next year. I mean, look at Michael, when it came to parenting, obviously I was a natural.

The comparing began even before Joey was born. The pregnancies were so different, I was convinced Joey had to be a girl. I'd had horrible morning sickness the first four months of Michael's pregnancy, was on bed rest the last two months because of high blood pressure, and was anemic. I had no such problems with Joey, and was convinced it was because he was a girl, and there weren't any male hormones floating around throwing my body out of whack. I was shocked when he was born a boy. So much so, I joked that I wanted to check under the delivery table and make sure the Doctor hadn't switched babies, but Joey was the spitting image of his Dad, so I knew he was really mine.

Joey was a very affectionate little baby. I called him my cuddle bug or Joe-Bug for short. He would just melt into my arms and play with my hair, twisting it around his chubby little finger, until he had tied it into knots. Still, he was so sweet about it, I couldn't help but let him do it.

It wasn't long before I noticed Joey liked all hair, and would cuddle with anyone who happened to walk through the door. If they had silky smooth hair, he was in their lap cuddling within a few minutes of them entering the room. He was so sweet about it, everyone let him. We also bought him baby dolls with long hair and he'd carry them around playing with their hair until it was too matted to twist, and then he'd need another doll.

It wasn't until Joey was born that I noticed how independent Michael was, or how clumsily he seemed to cuddle compared to Joey. Michael obviously loved us, but wasn't as good at demonstrating it as Joey. Joey was a natural.

Joey couldn't sleep through the night. Every two hours for the first nine months of his life, he'd wake up and cry. I'd come running, and rock him back to sleep, over and over again. Finally, I talked to his pediatrician about it, and he said it was my fault because I was rocking him to sleep with a pacifier in his mouth. When the pacifier would eventually fall out, he'd wake up, and since I'd always rocked him, he didn't know how to put himself back to sleep. He told me to get him ready for bed, read him a story and say his prayers, and then put him in bed without a pacifier, leave the room, and let him cry himself to sleep. He said, no matter what, don't go back in that room until morning. The first night, I felt like climbing the walls outside his room. He cried for twenty-seven minutes before drifting off to sleep. The second night, it took him nine minutes of crying to fall asleep. After that, he could go to sleep on his own and sleep through the night.

Joey was such a little sweetheart until he hit his Terrible Twos. He definitely lived up to that name! Where Michael just did whatever I asked, Joey put his little hands on his hips and asked, "Why?" From the moment he woke up until the moment he went to sleep, the entire day was spent in a battle of wills. He didn't accept my authority over his life. Everything I asked him to do, had to be logically analyzed. If he decided my logic outweighed his logic, then he'd go along willingly. If he thought his logic made more sense, he planted his little feet and would do a very convincing impression of an immovable object. Every night that whole year, as I dropped into bed, exhausted, my prayer was the same, "Please, God, tomorrow, don't let that two year old beat me." I didn't realize it at the time, but what I was witnessing in my two boys was two different types of Autism.

After twelve years of marriage, Michael was six years old, and Joey was four. We'd experienced four hardship tours to South Korea. The first three times, I'd gone with my ex-husband, Michael had been there twice and Joey once. The fourth tour, our plane tickets would have been too expensive, and we had to spend the year living apart. By that time, I was aware of some major issues in our marriage. I felt the Military lifestyle definitely contributed to them. For the first time, I had options. I had moved back home for a year, and lived in the same town as my parents. I had a job and a few friends of my own. When My Ex-husband talked about re-enlisting again, I let him know that if he did, this time he'd be going alone.

My ex-husband left the military, and came home to live with us. He got a job at a Mom and Pop camera store as their assistant manager. It wasn't long until the elderly Mom and Pop were grooming us to buy the store from them when they retired. I quit my job so I could come to work with him. They taught us how to run the biggest camera store in town. Within a few short years, they handed over the reins.

The next few years were almost unbearable. We were both working eighteen hour days, trying to keep up production in the mini-lab. Back then, your photo processing was where all your profits came from. I had to replace their daughter as lab manager. She had over twelve years experience and I had none. Quality couldn't go down, so product waste and production time went way way up.

I had to throw away picture after picture until I got it right. It took me eighteen hours to accomplish what she had done in eight. We didn't want to be separated from our kids that long, so we put video game consoles and foam chairs that converted into sleeping mats in an upstairs office. Michael and Joey became the official store mascots. They had expensive toys, but very little attention from us. We would eat meals together in the upstairs break room, but it was always fast food from one of the restaurants nearby.

As the largest camera store in town we had thirteen employees, a mini-lab and a custom lab. Our store front carried gifts, photo frames, every camera from professional to snap-shot, photography equipment like back drops, filters, lights with stands, film projectors and more. We had it all. We were members of the Chamber of Commerce, and attended "Business After Hours" and other networking opportunities. Everyone wanted to know more about us and where we lived.

The truth was we lived in an old single wide trailer in a trailer park. We were embarrassed of our modest home. We feared people wouldn't do business with us if they knew we weren't as rich as them. We quickly sold our trailer, and bought a huge Acadian style home in a fancy sub-division. It was a beautiful home with a front porch swing, and a great room with a wall of windows looking out into a landscaped backyard complete with a kid's fort, above ground pool and privacy fence. The walls were twelve feet tall, and required actual art. Anything smaller than sixteen by twenty, looked like a postage stamp on those huge walls. We had to buy new furniture, and the style of the rooms pretty much dictated the style of the furniture. By the time I'd decorated it, we'd incurred much more debt.

The house was beautiful, but it wasn't homey. I felt like a curator of a museum. I never felt like I belonged there and half expected someone to show up and tell me to get out! It's miserable pretending to be someone you are not. At least it was for me; I felt like we lived in a neighborhood of frauds.

Every home in the neighborhood, including our own, had a completely stocked bar. As soon as you entered their home, they'd ask what you wanted to drink tonight. They kept refilling your glass as long as you were there. Then we'd exchange pleasantries like:

"How was your fourth quarter?"

"Great. How was yours?"

"Never better."

"What are your projections for next quarter?"

"We're seeing nothing but growth. And you?"

"Things are so great, we're thinking of expanding."

"That's great!"

Blah…blah…blah… The whole time we were drinking like fish and lying through our teeth. No one wanted to be the one to say business was down. I made the remark to my husband, "If we are all so happy, why does it take this much alcohol to keep this neighborhood running smoothly?" I quickly tired of the stuffy socializing. It wasn't long before my husband started attending the block parties alone.

The boys were so sweet and adorable at that age. I remember a super cute thing happened when Michael was in first grade and Joey was in kindergarten. We were late for school, and I was in the drop off line. Michael told Joey, "We're running late today, Joey, so I can't walk you to your class. I'll have to hug you as soon as we get out of the car, and then we'll both have to run to our own classes, okay?" As soon as they got out of the car, they gave each other a hug real tight, before they ran separate directions.

I asked the teacher manning the line, "Do they always do that?"

She replied, "Everyday, your oldest usually walks the youngest to his class, and they hug real tight before he leaves and goes to his own class. All of us teachers love your boys! They are so sweet. Most siblings are jealous of each other." It was one of my proudest moments as a mom. I didn't teach them that love. I believe it was a gift from God, instilled in them to help them through the turbulent life they would soon experience.

Chapter 3

What Went Wrong

The strange thing about dysfunctional relationships, is that they often feel functional. There's just something a little bit off about them. As long as nothing serious happens, you could coast along in that lifestyle for years without even realizing how damaging it is to the parties involved. Then, when some big event occurs, it knocks your world off it's axis. Your current arrangement has no ability to handle a problem of that magnitude, and before you knew it, your life is permanently changed.

Mike and I were too immature when we got married, and always struggled with communicating well with each other, which was ironic considering I was a communication major in college. My professor had taught me a "Said, heard, thought, felt, statement that I tried to use on Mike. It went like this, "When you said, 'I'm on my way home. What's for dinner?' I heard, 'I worked really hard today. My dinner better be waiting when I get home and it better be something I like.' So I thought. "My day wasn't exactly easy! Why does he expect me to always cook and plan the meals? And that made me feel angry."

Mike immediately said, "I don't want to listen to a paragraph every time you have something to say to me! Don't try to use your communication crap on me!" I was also much more in touch with my feelings and seemed to be able to talk circles around him. He hated our little "Talks" because I was probably better at talking than I was at listening. He finally started bowing out of discussions by saying, "You don't want to discuss this problem. You want to talk my ear off until I agree that you are right and I am wrong!"

Mike had been raised in a military family, and believed in strict discipline. I started to notice something a little peculiar about the way Mike related to our sons. Michael looked and acted like me, and Joey looked and acted like him. From toddlers to early elementary, I began to notice Mike was a little harsher with his parenting of Michael than with Joey. It was as if the mistakes Joey made were kind of cute, and Michael's mishaps were down-right irritating! Looking back, I think he was seeing character traits of mine in Michael that drove him crazy, but instead of talking to me about them, he lectured away at Michael, and hoped I'd get the hint. Unfortunately, I didn't recognize the pattern until way later.

Our marriage was delivered a series of blows, that sent us into a tail spin. The first happened March 23, 1999. My Dad passed away suddenly. For as long as I can remember, my Dad was my rock. I was a Daddy's girl all the time I was growing up, and he always made me feel safe and loved. He died suddenly, from a massive heart attack at night. I didn't realize when we hung up the phone earlier that night, that it would be our final goodbye.

There were so many things I wanted to say to him and hear his responses back to me. I still needed his love and wisdom in my life! Grief engulfed me like a thick suffocating blanket, and I had no idea how I could ever be happy again. Mike didn't know how to help me through my depression and encouraged me to seek counseling because compassion wasn't his strong suit. Counselors have told me, when big stuff happens in your marriage, you have the opportunity to grow together, or to grow apart. If you help each other through, you grow together, if you both go to separate corners, to deal with your grief alone, it can tear you apart. Although we lived together, we began slipping apart.

We had also bought our camera store at the worst possible time, because Digital Photography had just come out, and was completely revamping the industry. Many Mom and Pop businesses folded as consumers were able to see their pictures without processing them. Film developing was where the profits were in Mom and Pop camera stores and we watched those profits dry up as we did everything we could to keep our business in the black. We worked long hours struggling to keep our business afloat. The more stress we experienced in our business, the more it overflowed into our married life.

It was about that time I noticed an interesting change in the way Mike related to his sons. He stopped picking on Michael, and started taking things out on Joey. The sweet little boy who could do no wrong, suddenly became the biggest mess-up known to man.

I think on a subconscious level, he was seeing traits of his own that he was ashamed of, and instead of facing them himself, he was trying to reprimand them out of Joey. Joey was a little too relaxed for his Dad's liking, and charming to the point of being manipulative. I noticed Mike was much more grumpy and moody, but I didn't really know what was up.

A few more months went by, things seemed more settled, and I thought Mike had solved his problem. He bought himself a fancy mountain bike and started riding seven miles before breakfast. Maybe that was to help handle the stress.

One morning we awoke to the alarm as usual. As I headed to the kitchen to make breakfast, and before Mike headed out the door for his morning bike ride, Mike said, "Um, I need to tell you something. I don't really know how to tell you this, so I'll just spit it out. We haven't been bringing in enough in deposits to pay all our bills for some time now. I didn't want to worry you, so I've been robbing Peter to pay Paul, so to speak, hoping I'd be able to figure out a way to make us solvent, but it's become quite obvious that isn't going to work out. We're going to lose the business, and then we'll probably lose the house. I just thought you should hear it from me." Then he walked out the door and got on his bike to go for his usual morning bike ride. To say I was shocked would be a huge understatement!

I peeked my head into each boy's room and told them it was time to get up, but I was preoccupied with my thoughts, and never made sure that they woke up and got moving. As if on auto-pilot, I went into the kitchen and started making our usual breakfast. I was completely absorbed in my own thoughts. Thoughts like "How is this possible?"

"What will this mean?" and "Am I dreaming?" floated through my head as I scrambled eggs, cooked bacon, and buttered toast. I barely heard Mike walk through the back door and head down the hall to take his shower. As he passed Joey's room, he looked in to see Joey still sleeping in bed.

In an unchecked rage, Mike transferred all his frustrations with the business onto that poor sleeping child, and in one quick motion he jerked him out of bed with a fist full of his night shirt and stood Joey up at the side of the bed, as he took a seat on his bed. Not letting go of his shirt, but rather using it as a handle to pull Joey closer to his face, Mike proceeded to yell at him, Drill-Sargent style. I quickly snapped out of my trance, and hurried down the hall to Joey's room. Not wanting to interfere between a father and his son, but wanting to protect my son too, I opted to silently glare a warning at Mike. I stood behind Joey, out of his eyesight as Mike continued to lecture our boy.

"If I've told you once, I've told you a thousand times." Mike bellowed, "You will never amount to anything because you are lazy. You hear me? You are lazy! Look at this room (Actually it was pretty clean for kid standards). Why don't you get it clean and keep it clean! You never want to do anything but lay around, sleep and play. You'll never amount to anything as lazy as you are, but you know what? It doesn't even matter anymore. Because I'm through with you! Did you hear me? I said I'm through with you!"

As tears rolled down my sleepy boy's face, I realized I'd made the wrong choice and failed to protect him. "Mike, can I talk to you alone in our room?" With a shove, he pushed Joey onto his bed, let go of his night shirt and followed me to our room.

As soon as we were behind the closed door, I tried to appeal to him. "Mike, I know you are upset today, but don't take it out on Joey! He's not even a teenager yet. You have to model God's Fatherly love. He hasn't even begun to do the things that will really get to you!"

"Cyndi, you don't get it." He kind of snarled. "I'm through with all of you! As soon as we are done talking, I'm going to jump in my SUV, and you will never see me again."

"Mike, I don't know what you've done with the business," I said, "But I do know you are going to have to stay and clean up your own mess, because I don't even know what the problem is, so I can't fix it. If you want the kids and I to leave, we will go, but you'll have to stay and clean up your own mess."

It was as if a little weight was lifted from his shoulders. He relaxed a little and said, "Where will you go?"

"I think I'll move back to Wyoming, where I grew up. I could probably stay with my sister, Regina until I find a job and get an apartment." I was only bluffing. I hadn't thought about our marriage breaking up at all. I was desperately trying to keep it together!

I'd never talked Regina and her husband Larry about staying with their family, and had no idea if that was even a possibility. Really, I just wanted to know if he'd be so quick to send us away if he knew the arrangements would be permanent. It felt like he was holding all the cards, and was playing games with the kids and my emotions. I thought maybe he wouldn't be so quick to throw us away, if he knew I could make decisions too.

"That's a great idea!" He said, to my horrified surprise! "If you move to Wyoming, you'll put enough distance between me and the boys that I won't take my emotions out on them. Then, I can buckle down and work to save this business, and you can move there and find a job. Whichever one of us is the most successful, the other can move to live with them, and we'll start over with a clean slate! What a great idea, Cyndi! I think you'll have saved our marriage!"

I naively, believed him, and called my sister to ask if the kids and I could live in her basement until we could find a place of our own. She and her husband agreed, and so we started making plans for the kids and I to move to Wyoming, in just a few weeks, during the school year. I thought after we were gone, he'd miss us and want us back. Either he'd ask us to come back or he'd move to be with us, but either way, I'd need a good job.

Within about a month I'd polished up my resume, packed what few things we could fit in my compact car's trunk, and the kids and I were headed to our new life. They went from little rich kids with their own rooms and privacy fenced in back yard with a swimming pool and tree fort, to being homeless, and living with their single-mom in their Aunt and Uncle's basement, overnight. At the time, we had no idea that they were autistic, but we soon found out that they didn't have near the coping or social skills they needed to be able to weather such a huge change in their lives.

The morning I was scheduled to leave, Mike cried and cried, but he wouldn't tell me why and he wouldn't ask me to stay. I'm sure now that he knew our marriage was over then, and part of him regretted the choice, but I didn't know it then, and even if I had it wouldn't have mattered. It takes two to make a marriage, and obviously, Mike was through with ours.

We got in the car and drove to Regina and Larry's house in Wyoming. When we arrived I set out to find work as quickly as I could. Finally, I found a job. After going to job fairs and applying everywhere that would accept an application for about a week and a half, I was accepted to be an assistant manager at a fast food Restaurant.

I couldn't wait to call Mike and tell him the good news. I thought this would give us options. If he couldn't get the business profitable, he could move up to be with me, and we could survive on my meager salary until he found something to help out. I was filled with hope as I gushed my good news over the phone. My hope was dashed as soon as I heard his reply, "That's great news," Mike said, "Because I've decided I don't want a wife and kids."

Those words felt like a knife, plunged deep into my chest. All I could think about was how deeply this would hurt the boys, as well. "Oh, no you don't!" I said. "I will not break their hearts for you! If you are going to abandon them, you are going to do it yourself, and to their face!"

I felt I needed to look composed before my boys got home from school. It would be a few months before they'd know our happily ever after was over, and I didn't want to break the news too soon. It seemed cruel to hide the truth from them like that, but I knew that if I told them, and they asked their Dad over the phone if it was true, Mike would say yes, and then he'd feel his obligation had been met. Our kids were so sweet and young. I thought for sure, if he had to look them in the face, he'd remember his love and change his mind.

I was so wrong! Mike showed up with a rented truck full of our stuff a few days before Thanksgiving. The day before Thanksgiving, he informed me that he would be leaving that night, because he had no intention of facing my family on Thanksgiving. Mike took the boys to breakfast at Joey's favorite Restaurant and informed them that he no longer wanted to be a part of the family, and then dropped them off at school. I couldn't even be there to help them deal with their grief, I had to open that day at work. After I got off work, we gave Mike a ride to the bus station and that was it. Mike resigned from being a member of our family.

Chapter 4

The Wyoming Years

Parenting isn't easy! One of the hardest things about it is the objectives aren't even well defined. Since Mike and I treated our kids like little trophies, they worked hard to preform. High grades, awards at school, clean rooms, and obedient behavior were highly rewarded with praise and recognition, so Joey did his best to impress us. We did a horrible job of showing unconditional love, and despite his best efforts, Joey's world came crashing down.

Joey had to give up his room, his swimming pool, play fort, and friends. He moved over a thousand miles away from his Dad, and found himself living in his cousin's basement. Looking back, I really shouldn't be surprised Joey was reluctant to start a new school. All his past efforts got him no where. Why even try?

The grades were divided differently in the new town, so not only did Joey have to start school in the middle of the year, he was in a different school than Michael. No more walking each other to class and spending recess together! When you add that to the fact that Joey felt like all his efforts to do well in school in order to please his Dad had been a complete waste of time, it's easy to see how his little third grade mind was ready to drop out of school!

The Panic of knowing I needed to get a job, and the heartbreak of our lives turning into a complete mess prevented me from putting myself into Joey's shoes, or even relaxing enough to hear him out. I had no money to get Joey counseling and no patience for a child who was thwarting my efforts to get him a better life! I'm ashamed to say, my solution was to dress Joey myself, force him into the car and take him straight to the principal's office. The principal certainly was not going to put up with his shenanigans!

She informed Joey that he could sit on the bench outside her office until he was ready to go to class, and then he'd owe her equal time serving in-school suspension during lunch hours once he complied. If Joey tried to leave, she'd call the police and report him as a run-a-way, and he'd have to go to the juvenile home and wouldn't be allowed to live with his brother and I anymore.

Joey spent two and a half days on that bench outside her office before his new teacher sat on the bench next to him and asked if he was bored. Joey replied back that sitting there doing absolutely nothing was, in fact massively boring. The teacher smiled at Joey and said "You know, you'd sit for the same amount of time in my class, but at least you'd have recess and things to do. Perhaps then you wouldn't be so bored, and we'd love to have you join us."

What she said made sense, so Joey got up and followed her to class. The Principle was true to her word though, and gave Joey over a month of detention for the 18 hours he'd sat on that bench. What a horrible way to spend his first weeks of school! Imagine what the other kids thought of him once he finally made it to class!

I've noticed something unusual about Joey; perhaps you might know someone like this as well. He refuses to be bullied! You can't force Joey into submission. He's willing to discuss and accept fair compromises, but when you try to force him to do anything, he'll resist, no matter what the cost, just for principle's sake.

I can't help but wonder, if most of Joey's problems would have been avoided if even one adult in his life hadn't let him down. It started with his Dad, and then one by one, we all crashed down, like dominoes. Parents, Teachers, Principles, Counselors, doctors, even the police, we all failed to give Joey what he really needed from us! He wanted someone to listen and to care. Joey needed someone who could help him make sense of his changing world, and no matter which adult he turned to, we all let him down. Even a Non-profit organization that specialized in finding kids mentors failed him, and really hurt Joey in the process. Someone came out and interviewed the boys to see if they could find suitable mentors for them. They asked all kinds of questions, and then told the boys we'd hear back when they found a suitable match. They promised they'd find a suitable male role model for them to hang out with. They never called us back.

A few years ago, a man stood up in our church and asked for mentors for that charity organization. Joey whispered to me, "I don't like that organization."

"Why? I've always heard they do great work," I asked.

Joey said, "Because they came and interviewed us, and said they were going to match us with the perfect mentors for us, and then we never heard from them again. The message I got from that, was I wasn't good enough. No one wanted me. I'd already been rejected by my real dad. I didn't need rejected by them too."

From the time we moved to Wyoming, it took me about six weeks to save enough to get us our own low income energy efficient apartment next to the only mall in town. Unfortunately, our independence came at a steep price. Being the manager of a fast food restaurant is rough. Only two people on staff were salaried positions, everyone else made minimum wage. Every hour we had to check what percentage we were spending on labor, and if that number was too high, we had to send someone home. The salaried people had to take up the slack. I also had food counts, orders and schedules that needed figured after my shift was done, before I was allowed to go home.

I was working six days a week, and my typical day was from five in the morning to seven at night. The boys were having to get up on their own, catch the bus, go to school, come home to an empty apartment, do their homework and feed themselves. By the time I got home, I was dead tired and only got to spend a couple hours with them before needing to go to bed so I could do it all again the next day.

If you do anything consistently enough, it becomes a habit. When life got really hard, I switched to auto-pilot mode. Conscious decision making required an amount of energy I just didn't seem to have. Knee jerk reactions became the normal behavior in most cases. Angry outbursts were met with angrier responses until someone stomped off.

One day I got into an argument with Joey, but that day I'd grounded him from his room because the boys shared a room, and kept all their video games there. It hadn't seemed fair to say Michael couldn't play any games because Joey had misbehaved so saying he was grounded from the room seemed like a simple fix, though in hindsight it had left him nowhere to go. He walked toward the front door, and I was afraid he'd run away so I pushed past him and leaned against the door so he couldn't open it.

To my shock and horror, trapping Joey in the living room of the apartment did not convince him to calm down. True to form, refusing to be bullied into submission, he walked over to the sliding glass door to the balcony, and stepped outside. Then without any warning, he jumped from our second story apartment to the ground and stomped off in a huff.

It was only an hour or so until sunset, and I feared someone might abduct or kill Joey. So I called 911 and asked them to help me find my son. I didn't have to wait long for the police to show up. He took my report, basically asking me why Joey got mad and left. I don't even remember what the argument was about. Most likely it was homework or school. Those were touchy subjects with Joey. Then the policeman told me that if I signed his paper that I would press charges, they would help look for my son, but if they found him, he wouldn't be coming home. He'd be headed to a juvenile delinquent home to serve his time, because running away was a crime. I was standing in the doorway, with the policeman holding the paper out for me to sign, and trying my hardest to figure out what was best for Joey. I didn't want Joey to get a criminal record, and I certainly didn't want him to have to spend time with other wild out of control kids in a jail like setting. Still, I was afraid for his life if we couldn't find him and bring him home fast!

As I stood there trying to decide what the best move to make was, Joey came walking up the steps, and innocently asked the Policeman, "What seems to be the problem, Officer?"

The Policeman told him, "You scared your Mom to death! She was really worried about you. She thought you'd run away. I was just here taking her report, and then I was going to put out an APB (All Points Bulletin) for your arrest! You'd have been arrested and taken to Juvenal Hall. You're lucky you came home when you did, son, because you just got a get out of jail free card! Your Mom really loves you, or she wouldn't have worried so much. You better not ever run off again, or next time you won't be so lucky!"

He ripped up the report, and told me to have a goodnight. He said he hoped that his lecture had scared Joey straight, and he left. It wasn't until years later that Joey told me, he'd never really left. He only went outside to sit on the hill between our apartment building and the Mall, so he could cool off from being mad.

After that, I was a little more afraid of the power the police could wield over my son and a little afraid to call them for back-up. They weren't exactly the friendly crossing guard they portrayed them to be when I was growing up. I never called 911 again, as long as we lived in Wyoming.

The boys have fond memories of the year we lived in Wyoming. I kept lots of microwavable meals and snacks in the house for them, and they would basically fend for themselves. They'd go to the mall several afternoons a week, after they finished their homework. There was a video game store that would let them trade their video games in for different used ones they hadn't played yet. I was too busy working to be much of a parent. We did have fun together on my days off. We'd go out to eat, go to a movie or video game arcade, or find some other way to goof off together.

While we were in Wyoming, my Mom had moved to Michigan to live by my younger sister. She kept in touch with me over the phone and worried about the boys spending so much time on their own. She was afraid that without proper supervision, they'd make bad choices in their teenage years and wreck their chances at a good future. My Mom offered to help me raise the boys, and pay my way to move to Michigan where she and my sister, Tracey's family lived.

Chapter 5

Starting Over Again

Once again, I was homeless and out of a job. The first two months, we hid out in my Mom's Senior Citizen's Apartment. Residents were not allowed to be under the age of fifty years old. The boys and I were all too young to live there legitimately. We hid our things, entered through the side door, kept the noise down, and if anyone asked, we were "Visiting Grandma." Before too long, my Mom was afraid she'd get caught and be evicted, so we crashed on Aunt Tracey and Uncle Jim's floor of their apartment until better arrangements could be made.

The cost of living was so much higher in Michigan than it had been in Wyoming, I was afraid I'd made a huge mistake moving to Michigan. Apartments rented for a thousand dollars or more a month. I couldn't imagine how I could earn enough to rent one and feared we'd be out of the streets if Tracey and Jim's family got caught stashing us there. I've since learned that there are government programs available that could have helped me afford an apartment, and even go back to school to get trained for a good paying job, but programs don't help much if you aren't aware of them. I'm still not sure how you go about getting that type of help, but if you are in this type of trouble, I'd recommend Googling how to apply for Section Eight housing assistance, welfare, food stamps, and Pell Grants.

Finally, we found a used trailer for sale. I promised my Mom that if she bought it for me, I'd pay her two hundred dollars a month rent, along with the lot rent. That was much more affordable than any of the apartments we saw! Thankfully, my Mom agreed, and once again, we had our own roof over our heads.

It took a little longer for me to find a job in Michigan than it had in Wyoming. I finally got offered a job at a phone book company. I would have to pass a two week training course in a large city in Ohio to get that job. I wouldn't be able to come home for the weekend, but it was only for two weeks, and after that, my commute would be less than a one hour drive.

My Mom agreed to stay with the boys and start them in their new schools while I was away at training. We also got to move into our new trailer, so I hoped they'd be comfortable and do fine. I packed my bags and loaded the car to head to Ohio for training. Joey cried and cried when I told him goodbye. I said I'd be back in two weeks, but he said, "No, you won't! You'll die in a car crash on the way home. I just know it! That's how it always happens in movies." Secretly, I was afraid to go by myself, too. I'd never stayed at a hotel alone and was a little afraid of big city driving. I was facing my fears for the sake of my boys, but his comment cut me to the core! I told him not to worry, got in the car, and drove away, but I was nervous until I made it back home. What if, somehow, he was right about the fatal car wreck?

I studied hard at school and called often to check in. I talked to my Mom and the boys almost every night. It was an intense course, and my Mom and sister didn't want to worry me, so they didn't tell me how badly things were going at home. They knew I needed the job, and I had to pass the class to get it. After I got back, I found out the kids had refused to go to school eight of the ten days I was gone, no matter how hard my Mom begged them to go. So on top of having to deal with a new job, I learned my kids were well on their way towards being truant, and it would be imperative to get them to school the rest of the days and on time, regardless of how they might be feeling.

As luck would have it, once again they were in separate schools, but they did at least ride the same bus. They hated riding the bus to school, and didn't want to wait at the bus stop with the other kids, because they said the other kids were mean to them. I agreed to drive them to school on the way to work, so they only had to ride the bus home. When they got off the bus, they didn't hang around and chat with the mean kids, they went straight home. At least the afternoon part went well...

Mornings were tricky. More often than not, Michael and I dressed Joey ourselves, forced him into the car and held him in the back seat by using Child Safety locks to prevent him from opening the door. I'd drive to school and practically drag Joey out of the car and into the building. There, the school counselor would hold Joey while we ran out of the school, jumped in the car and drove away.

Once we were gone, since he had no where else to go Joey reluctantly went to class. Even now, it breaks my heart to think of how miserable his life was and that I'd subject him to that day after day, but I didn't really see what other choice I had. It was the law that you had to go to school, and I was so afraid if we didn't tow the line, and follow all the rules perfectly, the truancy officer would break down my door and haul my little bundles of joy away. I was sure they'd give them to a better more deserving family.

It was more important that we looked like we had a happy home than that we actually had one. If people at least believed I was doing a good job, they wouldn't take my kids away. That would buy me a little more time to figure this single parenting thing out so I could do it right.

Chapter 6

Miscommunication Based Bad Behavior

Joey always loved reading. When we moved to Michigan, one of our favorite things to do as a family every week, was to take a trip to the library on Saturday. We'd spend a couple hours there. The boys would be sitting in the Children's area looking at and reading books until they decided which three they wanted to check out that week, and I'd find a comfy chair in the periodical section and read all the articles in the Women's magazines that had caught my eye in the grocery store check out isles, but had been too expensive to buy for myself. Then I'd select one or two mind numbing novels for my weeks enjoyment, and we'd go home. It was a time we all looked forward to, and an outing that was free except for the gas it took to get us there.

This particular Saturday, Joey was really being defiant. I don't remember exactly what he did, but he probably just woke up in a cranky mood. He might have refused to do his chores, picked an argument with his brother, or refused to do his homework. Maybe he'd gotten in trouble with a teacher at school that week. I really don't remember, but it couldn't have been too serious. In a knee jerk, over reaction, I decided not taking him to the Library would be an effective punishment. Still, it didn't seem fair to Michael to make him skip the trip to the library when he'd been a model student and helpful son all week. Joey was at the golden age of twelve, where he theoretically could be left home alone. After one too many angry outbursts from him, I decided we'd leave him home to think about his actions, and go to the library without him.

We lived on the outskirts of a large city in Michigan. I worked in a town almost an hour away, and the boys went to school in a small town about half way between my work and our home. I always took the boys to that small town's Library. We'd found it on our way to drop them off at school, and since we drove that way everyday, it had kind of become our regular stomping grounds. It took about fifteen minutes to drive to the library, and most the time I was on fifty mile an hour roads. Michael and I drove straight there and back, but we were gone about two hours. I even picked out a few books I thought Joey would want to read that week, as a kind of peace offering. But, when we got home, Joey was gone! I instantly regretted my harsh punishment, and I remembered what happened when I called the Police in Wyoming.

I called my Mom, my sister, Tracey and her husband, Jim. Each of them drove every place they could think of to look. Michael stayed home in case Joey showed up, and I drove all round our neighborhood, and looked inside all the stores I knew we liked to frequent. As hard as I looked, it seemed as if he'd just disappeared!

It was getting later. Sunset was only a few hours away. The later it got, the more afraid I got. Why had I been so strict with him? I had swung by the house to check on Michael, when my cell phone rang. It was Tracey, "Jim and I found him. We're bringing him home now, and he's really sorry!"

I had never been so happy to see Joey alive and well, as when he jumped out of their car and ran to hug me and said he was sorry! I said I was just glad he was home, and asked why he left. Joey said after we left, he had time to think, and he really was sorry. Joey thought that since he was left home alone for being bad, and now that he was sorry, he wasn't being bad anymore, he didn't need to be punished anymore, so he decided to walk to the library to tell us he was sorry, so we wouldn't feel bad about it either.

Joey didn't know the way to the library, so he went to our corner gas station, and asked the clerk how to get to the library. There were lots of libraries in a city that big, and we'd gone to one in a neighboring town, but the clerk had told Joey about one in a kind of rundown part of downtown. Joey walked almost six miles to find out it was the wrong library, and had already made it about half-way back, when my sister found him walking home. By then, Joey was walking by the road we took to church every Sunday.

That was the second time I thought Joey "Ran away", and both times it was just miscommunication. As I write this now, I realize how unfairly life is stacked against kids in the first place. In Joey's eyes, he'd done nothing wrong. However, if I'd reacted the way I did in Wyoming, once again, this might have been enough to land him in a Juvenal Home for running away.

If you have an autistic child, it's important to remember they have a different thought process than you do. What I'd perceived as bad behavior, disobeying and running away, was actually Joey realizing his mistake and trying to seek forgiveness. Also, if I'd only realized the fear of abandonment that he had from the break-up of our original family unit, maybe I would have found a more compassionate reprimand then taking his only brother to do something fun and leaving him alone.

Autism Apparent

The more Joey's needs went unmet, the more his bad behavior escalated. I really didn't know what to do, so I called my big sister, Theresa for advice. I told her I was worried because he was very angry and leaning towards violence. I explained I was afraid to call the police, because I didn't want him to get a record, but I didn't know where to turn. She suggested counseling, but I said I was afraid he wouldn't be willing to go.

Theresa told me, "If you feel he is a danger to himself or others, or is gravely disabled (which basically means that because of a mental illness, their thought process is so mixed up that they can no longer meet their own basic needs of food, clothes, shelter and hygiene), you can call the police and tell them he's a troubled youth, and needs a police escort to Emergency Community Mental Health for a Psychological Evaluation. They will drive Joey to Emergency Community Mental Health for you, and it won't go on his record."

A few weeks later, it was a Sunday night, and Joey was getting more and more angry and agitated. All the sudden, he looked at me with this look like a deer's eyes staring into headlights. His eyes were wild, angry and seemed to look right through me! That look scared me and instinctively, my arms penned his in a bear hug, my leg swept his feet to bring him off balance, and I laid him face down on the carpet, and sat on his back. He kicked me in the butt, scratched my arms and pulled my hair, but I refused to let him get up. I asked Michael to bring me the phone, and after a slight hesitation, he did. Soon, the police arrived. After Michael let them in, I explained why I was restraining Joey. I explained I needed them to give him a ride to Emergency Mental Health. They hand cuffed him, supposedly for both his and their protection, put him in the back of the squad car, and had me follow them to Emergency Community Mental Health.

When we got there, Michael and I had to wait in the waiting room, while Joey was brought back to speak with the Doctor. After speaking with Joey for a while, and calming him down, the doctor asked to speak with me. He agreed Joey was a very troubled youth, and made arrangements for Joey to start having weekly visits with Doctor Bob.

One day, I came to Joey's school to pick him up for his appointment with Doctor Bob, and was surprised to see Joey already sitting in the front office. When the secretary saw me start to sign him out, she called for the principal. The principal said, "I'm glad you are here. I just tried to call you at work. We need to talk. Joey has been suspended for three days."

She explained, "Joey had a substitute teacher today. He wouldn't stop playing with another boy's school supplies, so the substitute told Joey to move tables to an empty one. When he refused to follow her directions, she told the other three kids at his table to move to the empty one, and they did. Unfortunately, Joey followed them to the new table!

Then the teacher told Joey to go to my office, but Joey refused. She grabbed his arm to try to make him go, and he grabbed her arm and gave her a friction burn for touching him. She looked out into the hall, and spotted two teachers talking, so she asked them to please escort him to my office. He kicked and screamed the whole way. After that much insubordination, I had no choice but to suspend him for three days! You may take him home now."

"Okay." I said, "I understand, and I'm sorry for all the trouble he caused. I'll have a talk with him." I went back to the waiting room, got Joey, and we left.

As we walked out to the car, I said, "Joe-Bug, what happened, Buddy?"

Joey said, "It was like this:

We had a substitute teacher, and I was messing with this other kid's ruler. He told me that if I didn't stop messing with his ruler, he was going to tell on me. I messed with it just a little bit more, and he stood up to tell on me.

I knew if he told on me, I'd get in trouble, so I put it back, and stopped messing with it. But he told on me anyway!

Then the teacher told me to switch tables, which was completely unnecessary, because I'd already stopped being bad. So I stayed where I was.

Then she told the other kids to switch tables, and they did. But our real teacher say's we're a team, and teams are supposed to stick together, so I had to go with my team!

Then she got mad at me and grabbed my arm, so I wiggled free and gave her a friction burn, because I have a right to defend myself, don't I?

After that, she got two teachers from the hall to escort me to the Principal's office, and they didn't escort me!

They dragged me, and that's not escorting. Is it, Mom?"

I waited until he was in his counseling appointment, and then I pulled out a paper, and wrote down word for word, exactly what he'd told me. The next morning, I told him to enjoy his day off at home, but I still stopped by his school on my way to work. I asked to speak with the principal. I told her I understood Joey was suspended, and I wasn't questioning her decision on that. "He is at home now," I explained, "But, yesterday, when we left, I asked Joey what happened, and I've written down his response. It really frightens me, because if I divorced myself from everything I know about rules and social hierarchy, this makes perfect sense to me." Then I handed her the paper.

She read it and sighed. Handing the paper back to me, she said, "Tell him to enjoy his days off. Don't punish him for them, but I can't revoke the suspension now."

"I understand." I said.

"And," She continued, "We need to have Joey tested for Autism." That was the first clue that things are not always what they seem.

Chapter 8

Unstable Living

It seemed as if our life was filled with polar extremes. We ate dinner together at the table every night. We went on nightly walks, and I read them chapter books as bedtime stories. Every Friday night, we had a pizza and movie night. We'd buy a carry out pizza for five dollars, a one dollar two liter of soda-pop, and rent two family-favorite (Which really meant old release) videos from the video rental store. We'd pop popcorn too, and sit on the couch together and watch movies.

All three of us looked forward to our "Friday Night, Date Night". It was such a special time for just me and my boys. Anyone who witnessed those moments would have thought we had a happy life, and I'd have agreed with them too. But we were living on a razor's edge of happiness, and a slight push from any direction, would send us toppling off into a dark scary abyss.

I never noticed there was a pattern to the times I called the police. I wonder if they did? Joey told me much later that most of his angry outbursts tended to happened on Sunday nights when he couldn't bear to face another school week. I wish I'd known that! If I'd made the connection, maybe we could have figured out a way to make the transition easier, or home-schooled.

As it was, over and over, I found myself riding Joey's back like a bucking bronco as he kicked, screamed and pulled my hair. Each time I asked Michael to bring me the phone, so I could call the police. I never thought about the pressure that put Michael under. It took seemingly ages for him to locate the phone and bring it to me, as he wrestled with whether to side with his Mom or his brother, who was also his best friend. Other than Joey's weekly outbursts, the only thing that would give away that something was wrong with our family to an outside observer was the fact that we had to have regular appointments with Joey's counselor Doctor Bob.

Joey really liked Doctor Bob. He had toys in the corner of his office, and Joey would sit in the corner of the room and play with the toys as Doctor Bob attempted to engage Joey in conversation. Often Joey would answer with only one word replies, or just wait for Doctor Bob to give up and talk to me. Doctor Bob didn't think he was getting through to Joey, or realize that he was giving me great advice on how to help Joey. I thought we were making some progress, but Doctor Bob didn't think so, especially when we kept calling 911 and going to Emergency Mental Health between appointments. Doctor Bob labeled Joey as Occupationally Defiant, and eventually gave up on ever reaching Joey.

When we went to our next appointment, Doctor Bob offered me some advice on how to handle things better in the future, feebly tried to engage Joey in conversation a few times, and then handed me Mary's business card at the end of our session.

He told me that I would no longer need to make appointments with him, because we'd advanced out of his program and now needed in-home care. Mary would be counseling us in our home from now on. I was kind of in a shocked daze as he put his arm on my shoulder and led me out into the hall, before closing the door behind me.

The finality of the moment hit me hard, and it seemed so unfair that others got to choose when we were no longer worth helping.

I stopped Joey, and took his hands in mine. "Do you understand what just happened?" I asked.

"What happened?" His sweet little face asked as his eyes scanned mine for answers.

"Doctor Bob isn't going to help us anymore. He thinks we need more help than he can give, so he's referring us to a woman named Mary, who will come to our house to meet with us, okay?"

"I liked Doctor Bob." Joey said as his eyes filled with tears. "Can I at least say goodbye?" My heart broke as I looked at my little boy who'd experienced way too many doors slamming in his face, for a kid his age.

"I don't know." I said, "But we can try." I knocked on the office door, and a surprised Doctor Bob answered it.

"Did you forget something?" He asked.

"No, but Joey didn't really understand what was happening when we left, and when I explained it to him out in the hall, he asked if he could at least tell you goodbye."

"Oh, okay." He said.

Joey lunged forward and bear hugged Doctor Bob as tightly as he could. He seemed so small next to that giant man, and clung to him dearly. With a surprised look on his face, he looked over Joey and said to me, "I didn't even know I was getting through to him at all."

Then the hug was over and we turned and walked out of his life.

I often wonder how life would have been if Joey had been better able to express himself, if people wouldn't have given up on him so easily, or reacted so harshly to his calls for help. Remember, as frustrating as it is when people you care about lash out, they are probably even more frustrated or they wouldn't be lashing out in the first place. I don't think anyone gets up in the morning and thinks, "I hope I can get into lots of trouble today, getting punished and yelled at is so much fun! It just would not do to let even one person be proud of me for what I do today."

Punishments are simply a deterrence. The threat of consequences is intended to make people stop and rethink their actions, but that only works if the person in question can see a better option. If they consider their current circumstance to be worse than the punishment, or they can't see any other options the nature of punishments changes. At that point the punishment simply becomes a risk that is worth taking for the chance that something might change. Punishments become oppressive as they are handed down from on high by people in authority, with a seeming lack of compassion. In such cases punishment loses its effectiveness.

You've likely heard the saying desperate times call for desperate measures, given a lack of better options it is no wonder that people who are at the end of their rope will not hesitate to break rules, or lash out. If we as individuals, and as a society would realize that more often, and if we were willing to understand that we are dealing with people who may have limited means of communication that have unmet needs, we'd get a lot farther in helping people work out the problems in their lives. While punishment has limited effectiveness people in need rarely turn away aid. Compassionate actions, and a willingness to forgive can bring peace, and joy into a life that previously had none.

Chapter 9

The Difference Between a Need and a Want

Even though Mary only came to see us once a week, she told me I could call her any time, and I frequently did throughout the week when I had a question about how to handle Joey. She would often tell me that Joey was just misbehaving to get attention, and that I should "Remove the audience" when he misbehaved. What she meant by that was when he was being bad, I should send him to his room and if he refused to go to his room, I should lock myself in mine or go outside. She thought that by removing the audience, he'd have no more incentive to act up, and then I could come back later and talk to him after he'd cooled down.

Problem is she was kinda right, but at the same time very, very wrong. That turned out to be pretty horrible advice for our situation. Joey was seeking attention, but it wasn't because he wanted attention, it was because he needed attention. I know that sounds like a small difference but it is a big deal. You see, if he just wanted attention, ignoring his misbehavior would have taught him getting attention that way was more trouble than it was worth. Eventually, he would have found a better way to seek my attention. However, since he needed my attention, not getting attention was simply never an option.

If I turned on the TV, he'd turn it off. If I looked away, he'd walk around me to get in my face. If I talked to someone else, he'd yell over my conversation. If I went to my car, he'd stand behind it so I couldn't leave without running him over... When someone feels like they need attention and they are will to do whatever it takes to get it, you can't look away! There is simply a practical limit to how far you can retreat. When they are willing to burn the world to get you to pay attention.

One time, when Joey was really mad, he grabbed a meat carving knife. I asked Michael to call 911. Michael looked visually upset, and said, "I can't." I locked myself in my room and asked Michael to bring me the phone, but he said he didn't think he could do that either. I asked Michael if he could go to my Mom's house and ask her to call 911 and he said, "No." "Can you at least ask Grandmother to come here?" I asked. "Yeah," Michael said. "I think I can do that." and he ran out the back door.

Meanwhile, Joey was telling me to come out of my room. I was afraid to face him when he had that huge knife. What I didn't realize was the factor that was inflaming his rage was he couldn't stand me walking away when he got angry. He desperately wanted to be heard, and the more I walked away from him, the angrier he got. With Michael out of the house, and me locked behind a closed door, Joey completely lost it!

He banged all over my hollow door, begging me to come out. Since the sound of pounding on a braced portion and a non-braced portion of a hollow door sounds noticeably different, and the top of the door would flex more when hit it, he figured out I had sat down on the floor. He knew I was blocking the door, intending to wait out his temper tantrum. It wasn't the first time I'd sat behind that door, but Joey decided that it would be my last.

He put the knife down, as he kicked and beat on the first panel of wood, and tore it away. Then he picked up the knife, and plunged it through the final piece of wood well above where he knew I was sitting. I was so afraid to see that huge blade plunging through the door and into my room above my head! I shoved my dresser in front of the door, and ran to the bathroom inside my room and locked that door. I felt like I was living a horror movie! I just knew within moments my son would be breaking through that door as well, to murder me. I couldn't understand what was taking Michael and my Mom so long to come, and envisioned them arriving to see me bleeding out into a pool of my own blood. It felt like hours, but it was really about twenty minutes they'd been gone already.

Joey destroyed my door that day, but after looking at the damage he'd done, instead of charging through the door to murder me like I thought was going to happen, he threw the knife toward the kitchen counter, sat on the floor, buried his face in his knees, and bawled like a baby over what he had done. When I heard him cry, I unlocked the bathroom door and the bedroom door he'd shattered, kicked the knife away, and came over to him and we held each other as we sat in the floor and cried. We both told each other how sorry we were that we'd let it come to that.

We'd barely finished hugging it out and getting to our feet, when my Mom and Michael walked in. As they observed the damaged door, I couldn't help but notice my Mom was all dressed up with her coat and purse. She said Michael had come over and said, "My Mom wants you to come over."

My Mom had guessed that I was inviting her to go somewhere fun with us. She had Michael wait for her as she changed clothes, touched up her make-up, and fixed her hair. He obediently waited without uttering a word about it being an emergency, or could she please hurry. When she saw the state of my house, and realized what had been happening as she changed her clothes, to say she was shocked would be an under statement.

I took down my shattered door and put it in the mobile home park's dumpster to destroy the evidence. Then I got rid of every knife sharper than a butter knife from my kitchen in an attempt to keep Joey safe. It made cooking more difficult, but it was a sacrifice worth making to know that Joey was safe. It turns out that was a false sense of security, since Joey had bought himself a pocket knife that he would play with when I wasn't around. He never used it during his temper tantrums, so I didn't find out about it until years later when the boys were joking about how absurd it had been to throw away all the knives we used to eat, but let Joey keep his pocket knife. Even if it wasn't an effective strategy, I needed that false sense of security to give me a bit of piece of mind.

Joey was acting up because he wanted to have some influence in the decisions that were spiraling his life out of control. "Removing the audience" was in a sense, sending him into solitary confinement which was the cruelest thing I could do. I do believe in counseling, and Mary helped me a lot, but it is important to remember that even the most qualified and well meaning counselor in the world can misread a situation and not all advice will be helpful. If it doesn't seem to be working perhaps a different approach will yield better results. In my case, since Joey was misbehaving to get attention, if I'd have paid more attention to him when he wasn't lashing out perhaps he wouldn't have felt the need to lash out in the first place.

Chapter 10

Losing Control

If you've ever had your child tested for Autism, you know what a struggle that is! Joey was diagnosed through the school system. They had an I. E. P.(Individual Educational Plan) team made up of the principal, the Counselor, the Speech Pathologist, a physical therapist, two of his teachers and me. The teachers and I filled out questionnaires. Mine was about home life, and theirs was about behaviors at school. Then the counselor, the school psychologist, the speech pathologist and physical therapists all did their own assessments of Joey, and together they came up with a diagnosis, and an individual education plan. They presented it to me in an I. E. P. meeting, and I could either accept it, disagree but allow them to follow their plan anyway, or disagree and not allow them to follow the plan.

The school social worker and I had gotten into a habit of passing Joey off like a baton every morning. I'd drag him in the building at the same time everyday, and the counselor would be there waiting to restrain Joey while I high-tailed it back to my car and drove away. After I was gone, the counselor would release Joey, and he'd reluctantly go to class, since all other options were gone.

One day, after we'd begun the evaluation to find out if Joey was autistic, an autism expert came to evaluate the school, and witnessed our hand-off. She said it was abusive, and you could never physically restrain an autistic child. The counselor called me and told me we weren't allowed to do that anymore. The principal said if he didn't want to go to school, just let him stay home. Don't fight with him about it. After he missed twenty days, the truancy officer would haul him before the judge, and maybe then he'd change his tune. I believed her, and took her advice. More often than not, the next few weeks Joey chose to stay home when Michael and I went to work and school.

Finally, the letter from the Truancy Officer arrived, but it was addressed to me! The letter said Joey had missed fifteen days, and if he missed five more days, he'd be truant. Then both of us would have to appear before the judge, where I could be fined or even face jail time for failing to make my son attend school. I was furious! I called the counselor and told him I felt set up! That letter had my name on it, not Joey's! The principal swore that if it came to that, she'd go to court with me and testify on my behalf, but the counselor took it one step further. He said, "If Joey refuses to come to school, you call me, and I'll come get him and make sure he gets there!"

It wasn't long until Joey called his bluff. He absolutely refused to go to school! I called the counselor, and true to his word, he said he was on his way over. By the time he arrived, Joey had crawled under his bunk bed, and wedged himself against the far wall. After a few attempts at trying to talk Joey into coming out, the counselor dropped to his belly and crawled under the bed to get him.

Joey liked the counselor, and let him pull him out, but my boys had two white cats and we didn't own a vacuum. The carpet looked clean enough, but when the counselor stood up, his clean crisp sweater vest was covered in cat hair! I was horrified! At that moment I resolved to get Joey to school with out the help of the social worker from then on.

They did a very thorough job of testing Joey, but it took a long time, and I couldn't afford to let Joey miss any more days. Joey had just had it with school, and couldn't stand the thought of one more day. The final straw came one morning without any warning. It started out like a normal day, but quickly went from bad to worse. Joey insisted he wasn't going to school, and I insisted he was. I dressed him against his will, and Michael and I man-handled him into the backseat.

I had the child safety locks to keep him in once we got him in there, but it was Michael's job to sit beside him and try to calm him down. This time he was adamant that he was not going to school and kept struggling to get to the front seat, because he knew there was no child safety lock on the front passenger seat. Joey was shockingly good at jumping out of moving vehicles. He's done it more times than I care to count, and he has never wiped out or gotten seriously hurt. Still, it is terrifying to see your son casually hop out a car moving 40 MPH, and then just take off running.

That is why it was considered vitally important to keep him in the back seat. A task that Michael had to wrestle with him basically the whole way to school to achieve. The closer we got to school, the more desperate Joey became to keep us from going there. Joey lunged forward, and reached for steering wheel in what appeared to an attempt to make me run into on coming traffic. I said, "Joey, knock it off! We could wreck and die!"

Joey said, "Good! Life sucks! I don't want to live anymore, but I don't want to make you guys sad when I'm gone, that won't be an issue if we die together!"

Michael fought harder to pin his arms so he couldn't do that anymore, but Joey kicked his leg forward and kicked the gear shift in the front seat sending it into neutral. Luckily I was able to put it back in drive, but it scared me out of my wits!

We were about two blocks from school when it happened. As soon as I pulled into the school parking lot, I parked in the fire lane, and called 911. The police were there within minutes and hauled Joey out of the car, cuffed him in front of all the school kids who were staring as they headed into the building, and put him in the back of their squad car. Then they and I headed to Emergency Mental Health.

At Emergency Mental Health, The doctors said there's a fine line between suicidal and homicidal. Once you've stopped valuing your own life, it's easy to stop valuing other's lives as well. They decided to have Joey committed to a mental hospital for evaluation. I didn't have a choice. Trying to wreck a car is a crime. Either he could go to the mental hospital, or he could be prosecuted as a juvenile, but there was no way he was going home this time.

The doctors also decided that Joey would be traveling to the Mental Hospital in the back of an ambulance. Since he was trying to wreck my car, it wouldn't be safe for me to drive him there. The nearest Mental hospital was hours away. Ironically, Michael got to skip school that day, because he had to ride with me to the Mental Hospital to admit Joey. I couldn't drive there and be back in time to pick up Michael from school, and I didn't even have time to take Michael to school anyway, because I had to follow behind the ambulance, sign the papers at the hospital, and give them my insurance card. So Joey got stuck in the mental hospital and Michael got a medical excuse to skip school that day.

Chapter 11

The Difference a Friend Can Make

The next ten days were pure living hell for Joey and me. The most painful thing I've ever endured was to watch them lock Joey away in a mental hospital, and send me home. I was only allowed to visit him twice a week for two hours, and I drove two hours there and two hours back to be able to do that. The only thing Joey had to give him comfort when he was there was a little stuffed toy lamb that he named "Baa Baa". Joey had him in his book bag when they took him into custody, and they let him keep it with him to comfort him. He looked so small and vulnerable, and I didn't want to leave, but they gave me no choice. Deep inside, I hoped and prayed that with some combination of counseling, therapy and medicine, they'd help him regain control of his life and he'd want to live again. That wasn't exactly what happened.

Once, when I called, I could hear him in the background arguing with nurses, then a struggle, him crying out, then a thud, and then nothing. I asked the nurse on the phone what they were doing to my son, and she said he refused to take his medications, so they wrestled him to the ground and sedated him.

After they sedated him, they tossed him onto a hard foam mat in the middle of a concrete room with no windows and locked the door. The rough landing had given him a bloody nose and there wasn't anything in the room for him to stop his bleeding with, so he just laid on the mat in an ever growing pool of his own blood. Eventually he got bored and started finger painting with his own blood while the nurses watched him through the security camera. That is what he was doing when I called back 30 minutes after he had refused to take his medicine. The nurse complained about the mess, and said he'd have to get him and clean him up. I should call back in thirty minutes, if I wanted to talk to Joey.

Joey and I both made sacrifices for each other to show our love during that difficult time. Aside from the trips up to visit him, I took care of his virtual pet while he was gone. He'd been playing a video game online. He had a virtual pet that needed fed and played with on a regular schedule. He gave me his log-in password and made me promise I would care for his pet and not let it die. I'd hurry home from work, and feed, and play with that virtual pet as if it were a live one. Joey was counting on me to take care of it, and I didn't want to let him down.

As for Joey's sacrifice: things were going pretty well at work. Our area managed to meet the financial goal for the advertising in our phone book. The managers planned an evening out as a team to celebrate. They rented us two stretch limo's to take us to a popular casino a few hours drive away. They treated us to Chicago style pizza at a restaurant across the street, and then we all went to try our luck on the machines in the casino.

The date they picked for the party, just happened to be my birthday, and one of the two days that I was allowed to visit Joey. When I told Joey about it, I told him I was going to skip the party so I could come see him instead. I was a little afraid it might come back to bite me that I skipped a "Team Building" activity at work, but I couldn't imagine going, knowing that Joey was there without visitors. But Joey said, "No, Mom. I want you to go and have fun. That will be my Birthday gift to you. I want you to call me the next day and tell me all about what it's like to ride in a Limo." He insisted, so I went, and that was such a sweet selfless gesture he gave to me.

Two days later, the hospital called me in for a meeting to let me know how he was doing. When I got sat down in the Doctor's office, he simply said, "You can take Joey home today."

"Is he better? Did you convince him not to be suicidal? Are you sure he'll be able to handle his life now?" I asked hoping our problems would finally be over.

"No, but your insurance only pays for ten days. It's been ten days now. We charge one thousand dollars a night for a bed here, so unless you can pay one thousand dollars a night, it's time to take Joey home." The Doctor replied. Words can't describe the level of disgust and regret I felt when I heard those words! There may be some good mental hospitals somewhere, but that certainly wasn't one of them!

When Joey got back to school, they finished his evaluation. All the tests pointed to him being autistic, but they said they weren't sure because he was having so many emotional problems at the time. They chose the lesser label of emotionally impaired (E. I. for short), instead of Autistic Impairment (A. I.), because he could outgrow an E. I. label, and an A. I. label is for life. They hoped that when his emotional stress went away, his symptoms would too. They were wrong, and it was a bad choice to make.

Turns out many schools label defiant children as E. I. so they have the opportunity to move them to Special Education classrooms and get them away from the rest of the class. My experience was most teachers show compassion to autistic children, and want to punish E. I. students into submission. To get through the rest of the year, Joey was allowed to be picked up at home by the Special Education bus, and do all his schoolwork in the "Fish Bowl" under the guidance counselor's supervision.

The fish bowl was a glass room in the middle of the main hall, where students could be put for in-school suspension. It was supposed to be punitive, because all the other kids could see you were being punished. Joey however preferred it to his actual classes because it was a small room with only three desks and no one was allowed to talk in it so he was free to finish his work at his own pace and then read a book or take a nap until time to go home. He thrived in that setting. Unfortunately, he aged out of that school that year, and the next year he had to start all over at Michael's school.

His first day of school at Junior High, I couldn't even get Joey to get out of the car. After several attempts of talking him into going into the building failed, I had Michael sit with him, while I went in to talk to the principal. I explained that Joey was in the car refusing to come into the building. He called Joey's home room teacher, a Special Education teacher, and asked her to go out and talk to him. Michael went to class, and she asked me if it would be okay for her to sit in my car. I said okay, and she opened the passenger's side door and sat in the front seat.

Looking back into the backseat, Mrs. R. introduced herself to Joey, and told him how excited she was to have him in her class this year! Mrs. R. described how she'd decorated the room, and even had a wall with all the names of "Her kids" on it, and Joey's name was on there too. Mrs. R. had a reading corner with good books and comfy chairs, and she was sure Joey would like her class, if he just gave it a try.

Mrs. R. said she was sure they were going to be great friends! She said, "I really want you to see our room, Joey! How about if you come with me for two hours, and I'll get your Mom's cell phone number. If you don't want to stay after two hours, I'll call your Mom at work, and ask her to come bring you home. Would that be okay, Joey?"

Mrs. R. was amazing, and worth her weight in gold! She made him feel accepted and even wanted, and he willingly got out of the car, and followed her into her class. He didn't choose to leave early that day, and made a smooth transition to that school. It was mostly thanks to that teacher.

Unfortunately, he didn't make any friends his age, except for one little boy who needed a wheelchair to get around. They were best friends at school, but never really got to hang out together outside of school. That year we had Joey's birthday party at an arcade dinner, and he invited everyone in his class. Joey's friend was the only one who showed up, but he and his Mom were 45 minutes late, and didn't call to tell us they were running late.

The first 45 minutes of his party, Joey sat at a table staring at the door, refusing to eat pizza, cake, play games, or open presents until his guests arrived. Eventually Joey broke down into tears when he thought no one was going to come, but the moment he saw his friend wheeling up to the door he wiped the tears from his eyes, and ran to go meet his friend with a smile beaming on his face. Even though his friend was late, it made Joey's night that he came.

It really goes to show that you don't necessarily need to do much to make someone happy. Sometimes it is enough to make time for them and be there for them when they are counting on you. That kid will probably never know how big a difference his showing up made that night, because he didn't see what the party was like before he arrived, but the difference between having no friends and one friend was like night and day.

Chapter 12

Dating in Secret

Along with being too busy with my work, and completely misunderstanding what Joey was going through with school and failing to meet his needs, I also broke my promise to my boys to stay single and I started dating. Don was my knight in shining armor. When I was assigned my first batch of accounts from the phone book company, Don's drain cleaning company was the one that caught my eye the most. He had a funny little logo and a kind of silly tag line. I was impressed with anyone who was so self-abasing that they could make jokes about themselves getting dirty cleaning your toilet!

I practiced on Don's account at my training in Ohio, and couldn't wait to call him for an appointment once I graduated and got the job. The day I called Don was the one year anniversary of his late wife's death. He told me his wife died and to call back later.

I was shocked because I thought he meant she had passed away that day! My heart went out to him immediately. I was still grieving the loss of my Dad and the loss of my marriage, so I hurt for anyone I saw experiencing loss.

I was always taught that if your spouse dies, you shouldn't start dating until they have been gone a year, out of respect for them. I believe God had me call Don on the one year anniversary of her death as a hint that we were supposed to be together. His family and friends had been encouraging him to date again, but so far he hadn't met anyone who was a good match. Then I called, but he wasn't in any mood for business decisions and told me to call back later.

I had to meet with my boss every Monday morning, and let him know how my revenue accounts were doing and what appointments I had scheduled for the week. I was required to touch base with each of them weekly, and get them signed to a new contract for that year as soon as possible. Then I was also supposed to be finding new accounts, and any accounts that dropped out of the book, I was required to replace with a new account of at least equal value, so I didn't lose any revenue. If my schedule wasn't filled with appointments for the week, my boss would make me reschedule the day's appointments, and stay in the office to make prospecting calls under his supervision.

Since I was required to call Don every week, and both of us were going through some difficult times, we got to be pretty close friends over the course of a few months. Unfortunately, my boss wasn't near as understanding of what Don was going through, and was more concerned about not losing revenue for the book. After about a month and a half of calling weekly and meeting for coffee several times, Don still hadn't renewed his contract, and my boss threatened to take away his account if I didn't get him to sign that week.

I thought everyone else had left for lunch, as I sat worrying about what I should do. One of the more successful seasoned executives walked into the room, and when she saw me looking distraught, she immediately asked what was wrong. I told her I couldn't afford to lose that account. Don's was my biggest one! If I lost it and couldn't replace it, I'd lose my job! I really needed the medical insurance for my son. She said, "Whenever I can't get someone to sign, I invite them to lunch. Once I've bought their lunch, I can usually guilt them into signing. Try that."

I didn't want to play games and I hated being under-handed, but I really needed my job so I could support my boys. This felt like my only option. I made the call. "Hi, Don. This is Cyndi, your yellow pages rep. I was wondering if I could buy you lunch this week."

Don kind of chuckled and said, "Cyndi, I'm fifty-two years old, and no woman has ever bought me lunch! I'm not about to start that now! If you are hungry, I'll feed you. When and where do you want to meet?" We decided to meet Wednesday at three PM at a restaurant in the mall.

Then I said, "Don, I think it's only fair to tell you, my boss said I have to get you to sign your contract this week or he's going to take your account away from me."

"Well, we better get it done then," Don said. "I'll see you Wednesday, and don't forget to bring those papers." Then we said our goodbyes and hung up the phone.

On Wednesday, we'd no sooner been seated and the waitress had taken our drink order, than Don said, "Well, let me see those papers. Let's get that out of the way." He signed the papers and just like that, our business meeting turned into a date. We spent the meal talking about how he was starting to date again and had just met someone, but they'd only dated once and he could break it off if I was interested.

I told him I promised my boys not to date because they needed me and we'd all been hurt too badly when their Dad left. After lunch, he walked me to my car, and said, "Well, if this is really goodbye, give me a hug." and hugged me tight. I watched as he walked away, and once he was gone I got in my car and drove away.

But it wasn't really goodbye. I'd often think about him, and call to see how he was doing. Don, in turn, would ask how my boys were doing, and drop of christian books he thought might help me at work. We really cared about each other, and so it wasn't very long until we began dating in secret.

For our first official date we went to dinner at a fancy restaurant. I didn't want the boys to know I was dating Don until I was sure our relationship would last. I felt terrible sneaking behind their back, but I still felt they really needed a good male role model in their life, and I was pretty sure he could be that man. I told Don that I didn't want him to meet my boys until I was sure he and I made sense as a couple, because I didn't want my boys to meet and lose every guy I decided to date.

I lied to my boys and said I had to work late. It felt horrible lying to them, and breaking my promise not to date, but I justified it to myself by saying it was "For their own good." I drove myself to the restaurant and he was already there waiting for me. The waitress showed us to a little secluded table.

We had a wonderful dinner, chatted like old friends, and by the end of the evening, we were both convinced we were a perfect match for each other. Don walked me to my car. "Wait here. I have something for you." he said, and then he walked to his car, and pulled out a box containing a presentation bouquet of a dozen roses in all different colors. You know, the kind a beauty pageant winner carries after she's been crowned. I'd never seen such a beautiful bouquet of flowers, let alone been given one! That was a problem! I'd told the boys I had to work late. How was I supposed to explain the huge bouquet?

We had a new promotion going on at work. My boss at work had made a wheel with various awards like a free tank of gas, a gift card to a restaurant, or a day off with pay. Whenever we sold a new account, we got to "Spin the Wheel". I lied and told the boys I closed an account, spun the wheel and won the roses. I gave the box of roses to my boys when I got home. As much as I loved them, I didn't feel like I deserved them because I'd lied to my boys. Joey loved the roses. He got out every vase we owned, and separated the big bouquet into many smaller ones. He put his arrangements in every room of our house. He was so excited.

Don called me the next day and asked me if he could take me out again the following Wednesday. That night he set the pattern for what would become our dating ritual. About noon on that Wednesday, and every following Wednesday, two bouquets in vases arrived at my office. There were a dozen roses for me, and a dozen multicolored carnations for the other girls in my office to share, "So they wouldn't be jealous." I'd also receive a note saying he was looking forward to our date that night.

Those two weekly bouquets arrived at my office every Wednesday as long as I worked there, and my female co-workers looked forward to them as much as I did! After work, he took me out to dinner. We tried a new fancy restaurant every week, followed by the Wednesday night service at his church, then a movie, and then we'd go to his parent's house for coffee and conversation.

Chapter 13

A Pity Party is a Lame Party

When the time came that I felt he should meet Michael and Joey, I fixed dinner at home, and had him over to meet the boys. We rented a movie to watch at home with Michael and Joey. I told the boys I decided to date Don, but they hadn't really commented about how they felt about it. Joey was kind of quiet at dinner. I was busy worrying if my new boyfriend liked my cooking, and what he thought of us and our house.

When we popped popcorn and watched the movie, instead of sitting sandwiched between my boys, I sat on the couch next to Don, and he put his arm around me. Joey sat across the room in the chair, and kept looking at us all through the movie. I figured he was just getting used to Don. When the movie was over, I walked Don through the kitchen to the porch off the carport to say goodnight. Don was just about to kiss me goodnight, when the back door opened and Joey walked out.

To my surprise, Joey had followed us, and was watching from the window in the door as we said our goodbyes. When Don started to kiss me, Joey had decided it was time to intervene. "I think you need to leave. Now!" Joey told Don.

"I'll go when I'm ready to go." Don said. "I don't take orders from teenage boys!"

Joey pulled back his fist threatening to punch Don. Don picked Joey up, and carried him back inside. He sat Joey on the couch, and told him to stay there. When I walked Don back out to his car, I could see he was shaking. Don said, "I'm sorry for that, but I refuse to let a child intimidate me. I feel it's only fair to tell you, I'm not playing around. I'm looking for a wife, and I think you may be the one. I like your boys, and I think maybe we could be a family. I'm not going to let them bully me, but I promise I'll stay out of the way and let you discipline them yourself. I'd like to date you once a week so we can get to know each other. If we both agree this is right, we'll be married within the year. I think it's only fair to tell you, I have four grown kids, and ten grand-kids. Think it over. I'll call you tomorrow." Then he hugged and kissed me, got in his car and left.

My head was swimming when I went in the house. Joey was steaming mad! I told Joey I loved him, and held him in my arms. I promised I'd still love him forever, whether I remarried or not. He calmed down, and accepted my decision.

By now it was fall. A new school year had started, and Joey was in the same school as Michael. Joey had the nice Special Ed. Teacher I already told you about. Football season had also started, and Football was and still is a big deal to Don! Don was a season ticket holder for a local college football team.

About the third game of the season, Joey decided he had enough of me being gone every Saturday, and decided to stage a protest. Joey said if I left with Don, he wouldn't be home when I came back.

Since he'd taken off twice before, once in Wyoming and once when he went looking for the library, I had good reason to believe he'd make good on his threat. I also knew that if I went to the game, I'd be gone most of the day, and he could be long gone before I'd have the chance to look for him. I asked Don to take Michael in my place, and decided to stay home with Joey.

After they left, I didn't want Joey to feel like he "Won", so I sent him to his room for "Ruining My Saturday". Joey had enough, and rather than refuse like he normally would, he simply let out a howl of rage. Then Joey hung his head, and went to his room without saying a word. Then I went to my room to sulk. As I write those words, I'm filled with shame that I couldn't recognize his bad behavior as the desperate plea for my love and attention that it was. Instead of giving him discipline and rejection, I should have given him reassurance and a positive day together.

Joey had gone to his room covered himself with a blanket, and since I had punished him for demanding I stay home he decided to test to see if I still loved him. He reasoned if I cared I should come check on him at some point so he would make a really slow but completely quiet suicide attempt. If I came he'd stop, and if I didn't he'd die leaving me with guilt for having lied to him that my relationship with Don wouldn't stop me from loving him. He had a necklace that had a metal coin pendant attached to a pretty strong cord, so every couple of seconds he'd turn the coin over adding another twist to the cord it would take some time due to all the slack in the cord but eventually it would choke him.

Fortunately, my sulking turned into praying for direction, and in my mind I heard an urgent demand, "Go check on Joey!" By the time I'd arrived Joey was crying and struggling to breath, but he couldn't take the necklace off. Joey's plan had a rather major oversight: it turns out that twisting a necklace hundreds of times can get it pretty tangled up and it was knotted too tight for him to remove it.

I quickly ran to the kitchen, grabbed my scissors, and cut the string so he could breathe again. I hugged him tight, and we both agreed that we were glad I'd gotten there in time to save him.

Joey explained his plan, and how during the several minutes he'd spent twisting the necklace he'd thought better of it, but couldn't get the cord off because it had gotten tangled up. I really think God's Holy Spirit warned me to save my son that day, by telling me to "Go check on Joey."

After that I decided to go do something that would help Joey use his energy in a positive way. We decided to walk to Joey's favorite Chinese restaurant for lunch. We under estimated how far away it was, because we had only driven there before. After walking over four miles and not even being half way there, we called my Mom and asked her to pick us up and take us there, and we'd buy her lunch too. Thankfully, she did, and we enjoyed the rest of the day together.

Chapter 14

Vocalizing Fears

Joey's problems with school and the medications he was taking to handle them, began to cause me to have problems at work too. When one member of the family has problems coping with life, it has a tendency to spill over into the other member's lives as well. Especially if you are a single Mom. There's a saying, the buck stops here, and that was certainly the case for me. It started just like any other day. I was in my cubicle at work when the call came in.

"Is this Joey's mom?"

"Yes."

"Hello. I'm the school councilor. He's doing that hoodie thing again in History class. I'm afraid you'll have to come get him. None of us can get him to respond."

"I'll be right there." I grabbed my purse and keys, and peeked into my boss' office.

"I'm sorry, Fred. I'm going to have to work from home the rest of the day. The school called. They're having problems with Joey again."

"Alright." Fred said as he shook his head, "But you are going to have to figure something out about that!"

"I know. Thanks." I said as I headed for the door.

I wondered what it would be this time, as I pulled into the parking lot. The councilor was anxiously waiting for me in the office, and led me to the classroom. There was Joey, with his hoodie pulled down over his face, his face planted on the desk, and just like a little turtle who was unsure of his surroundings, Joey had retreated into his shell refusing to say or do anything. The teacher and the entire class looked nervous, and one boy stood hovering around, not sure what to do.

The councilor explained, "The bell rang, and classes changed before you got here, but Joey refused to budge. He's in that child's seat. We don't know what to do. We were hoping you could help."

I knelt down at his desk and tried to peek up into his hoodie. It was dark in there, but I thought I might have seen one eye. I spoke in a low comforting tone. "Joey, it's Mama here. How about we just go home? Do you want to go home with me, now?" He nodded his head a little, stood up, and walked to the door with his head down.

The teacher whispered, "It's amazing how you did that! He wouldn't respond to me."

I smiled at her as I put my arm lovingly around my son. "We'll be going now. Have a nice day."

"I took the pleasure of signing him out for you." The councilor said as we headed out the door. "No need to stop at the office. Thanks for your help. Enjoy your day, Joey!"

Her words irritated me. Did she really get pleasure out of signing him out, or had it just been a nice gesture to prevent Joey from experiencing any extra trauma in the office? And, "Have a nice day, Joey!?!" Really? Could she not see that this incident at the very least would warrant a call to his psychiatrist, maybe an emergency meeting and perhaps another medicine change? What's so nice about that?

As we got in the car and headed home, my mind was swirling with questions. What had prompted this? How long had he sat like that before they called me? Would I be able to keep my job when I kept having these types of issues? What was I doing wrong with raising Joey? Was it my fault? The schools? Kid's picking on him? Joey just being stubborn? As the thoughts churned around and around in my brain, one thought came tumbling out of my mouth, uncensored.

"Joey, what's going to happen to you? I mean, you can stay with me until I die, but I'm older and will probably die before you, and what then? How will you handle your world? What will happen to you?"

The words just hung in the air. I'd really said them, and I couldn't take them back. These were fears I wrestled with constantly, but I'd never voiced them before to anyone, let alone Joey and during the middle of a melt down! What had I done? What was I thinking? Maybe, I'll get lucky and he's so deep inside his own thoughts right now, he didn't hear me, I thought to myself. After all, he hadn't said a word since we left the school.

"I have to believe that God had some purpose in mind when he made me." Said Joey. "God packed my bag with everything I'd need for the trip when He created me. I just have to believe that I'll be alright."

Wow! It wasn't the first or last time that my son's faith humbled and convicted me. Okay, worry less and pray more. I got it. With that, we drove home in silence. Each examining our own thoughts.

Chapter 15

Happy Memories

In just a few short months, Don and I knew what we had together was real, and Don was ready to put a ring on my finger. I felt it was too soon for the kids to see me wearing one, so we put it on lay-a-way to give them a little time to get used to the idea. Shortly there after, Don took the boys shopping, "To give me a break." Michael and Joey each came home with a new toy, and the three of them had picked me out a birthstone ring as a symbol of all their love, and I wore that on my ring finger until I thought they were more ready for me to get an engagement ring.

Time moved on, and Don became a bigger and bigger part of our lives. Soon, we found ourselves celebrating Thanksgiving and Christmas. Ever since Michael was a baby, Black Friday Shopping was an important part of my holiday tradition. I believe that shopping the sales on that day, allows me to buy double the value of presents I give for Christmas, since everything is sold at such a cheap price that day to kick off the holiday season and get shoppers in the mood to shop.

There have been a lot of years in my life when money was tight, and I really needed those sales to be able to afford much at all. I really thought this year would be no exception. I was barely squeaking by with my Yellow Pages job.

Imagine my surprise when the night before Thanksgiving, Don placed fifteen crisp hundred dollar bills in my hand, along with a list of names and ages of all his grand kids, as well as their Mom's phone numbers. He told me I could use that money to shop for Michael, Joey and his ten grand kids, and I could divide it how I saw fit. I decided that Michael and Joey should get a double portion since his grand-kids also had parents to buy for them. I was so grateful that I didn't have to worry where my kids gifts would come from that year, and it was all thanks to him!

On Black Friday, I woke Michael before dawn to help me shop. We were sipping hot cocoa and standing in line at the toy store when they opened at five in the morning. We quickly filled two carts with toys and headed for the check out, Michael had worried each time I put another toy in the cart that it was more than we could afford, and maybe I was going over board. I hadn't told him how much money Don gave me. He was shocked when I paid the cashier with five crisp hundred dollar bills from the stack in my purse. We filled the back seat, and trunk of my car, and had to go home and unload before we could check out another store. Then, I dropped Michael off at home and woke Joey to go with me to get Michael's presents, wrapping paper and Christmas cards.

When Don came over after he got off work, our shopping was done. The tree was loaded with presents, and we were ready to focus on the Spiritual side of Advent to prepare our hearts for Jesus' Birth since all the commercialism was already covered.

You may be wondering why I bothered to include a cheery story about a favorite Christmas memory in this book about preventing suicide. The simple answer is the more you can include people you care about in creating happy memories, the more you can little by little improve their mood, and make them feel loved and appreciated. Anything you can do to help them feel loved, appreciated, or accepted is a step in the right direction.

Life wasn't perfect for us, and it won't be perfect for you either. But there will be magic moments for you to hold onto during rough patches. Beautiful memories like that amazing Christmas shopping experience are just the thing to remind you why all the hard effort is worth it. All the wonderful little memories you can string together are like flotation devices you and your loved ones can cling to. They'll help you weather the storms of life. Remember, suicide attempts are often pleas for help. Every time you let them know you are listening, you help alleviate a little of their inner turmoil and step a little closer to creating the kind of bond you both crave and need.

That Christmas, Don got my ring out of lay-a-way and put it on my finger. Soon we were planning a wedding for March, just a few months away. Unfortunately for the boys, that would mean yet another move to the town Don lived in and I worked in. I decided it would probably be a smoother transition to move during the semester break than in March. So once again, we found ourselves in the principal's office registering for a new school.

Chapter 16

Autism for Two

The first time Joey had to change schools after being tested for Autism in middle school was when he moved up to the Junior High where Michael was. That is when I learned that the E. I. label was often used to weed out problem children who were disruptive in class. That way, they could send them to smaller special education classrooms. There they could better handle them, and the students wouldn't be disrupting the children trying to learn. I found the E. I. Label worked against Joey, because he was highly intelligent, so most the classes he took were main streamed classes with all the "Normal" kids. The regular teachers would read that E. I. Label, and assume he was a problem child who required more discipline. They'd then give him even stricter treatment instead of the understanding and compassion he required.

I didn't want that to happen again when we moved to live with Don, so when I signed the boys up at their new school, I was sure to explain to their new principal that Joey was really autistic, and show him the results of all the testing they had done to prove it. I wanted to avoid that problem again. In just a few short weeks, the principal called me for a meeting in his office. He said the teachers wanted more advice on how to relate to my autistic son. I came to his office, and kept talking to him about Joey and Joey's needs, but he kept calling him Michael.

Finally, I said, "No, you have my sons mixed up. Joey is the Autistic one."

The principal replied, "Then we need to test Michael too, because the teachers are noticing all kinds of Autistic traits in him. For example, we store the pop for the vending machine in his science classroom. The first time Michael saw all the pop stored there, he counted how high, how deep and how wide the cans were. Michael did the math in his head, and asked his teacher, Did you know you have 484 cans of pop here? The teachers have also noticed that several of the girls found Michael attractive, and tried to flirt with him, but Michael seems oblivious to their advances. He also seems very awkward at trying to make friends. Michael doesn't seem to be able to read social cues at all."

I agreed to let them test Michael as well, and found that he too, was high functioning autistic. Michael tested at sixteenth grade level in math despite only being in eighth grade. Michael also had ADHD, Obsessive Compulsive disorder, and was completely incapable of asking for help when he needed it, or advocating for himself at all. Now I knew both my kids were autistic, but I still didn't know how to help either of them deal with their problems.

When your child is newly diagnosed with autism, it's easy to feel like life is spinning out of control. It's important to realize the opposite is actually true. Autism is present from birth. You just didn't know your child had it until now. So much like the lens of a camera, your world is coming more into focus, not less. He's still the same child you had yesterday before the label was applied. He didn't suddenly change. Now you just realize a little more why you have been struggling in the first place. The more you can learn about and understand your child, the better your relationship will be. The better your relationship is, the better his emotional well-being will be.

The label also affords you more help from the school and accommodations that may be essential to helping your child succeed in navigating the rough waters of middle and high school. Resist the urge to turn your child's life into your newest project. I must reiterate, they are the same kid they were yesterday. At least now you know what type books to read to get expert advice, but don't take those books as gospel truth. You might be more of an expert on your child than the experts because you've known him all his life.

I'm convinced the best person to consult when trying to help your child adjust to his life, is your child. The two of you can work it out. Relax, breath deep and talk it out. Little by little you'll find your way together, and it always helps if you pray for God's help as well.

Chapter 17

Medications List Side Effects For A Reason

I still remember Valentine's night, 2005. My fiance, Don and I had gone out for dinner and a movie. When we returned home, my older son, Michael was asleep in his bed. Joey was cowering in the corner behind Don's over-turned recliner chair. Joey's eyes looked wild with fear. He was sweating profusely. His hair was slicked down with sweat, and Joey's eyes were red and swollen from crying so hard.

As I knelt down and hugged Joey, he leaned into my embrace, and convulsed with sobs. Joey told me that Satan had tormented him all night long, and told him he either had to reject God, or kill himself.

Joey had fought that hallucination all night long waiting for me to get home. He was so relieved that I was finally home. I held Joey and reassured him that he would be okay. I prayed for protection over Joey, and put my precious son to bed.

The next day, I took Joey to an emergency appointment with his psychiatrist, and reported what he had endured the night before. The doctor asked Joey to go play in the waiting room while he talked to me. He recommended a strong anti-psychotic drug, one of the possible side effects of this drug was death. The doctor told me he wasn't choosing that drug lightly. Joey had attempted suicide four times, and was now hearing the voice of Satan.

He said this drug would shut up the voices inside Joey's head. The doctor felt without the drug, it was only a matter of time before Joey succeeded in committing suicide. With the use of this drug for a short time, and proper monitoring by his Doctor, maybe we could avoid it. I never felt so alone and scared!

I never even thought to check Joey's medications side effects at the time, I thought Joey needed those medicines to stay alive, so it probably didn't matter what the side effects were. Not taking them was a higher risk than anything that could be on those labels. I mean, what else would we do? Not take the medicine the Doctor thought would help? At that point I was beyond what I could handle. I had completely tunnel visioned in on medicine being the answer. If the Doctor believed it was best for him, then I trusted the Doctor.

In hindsight, however, Joey was taking several prescription drugs for his depression and anxiety at the time. One of the anti-depressants he was on has anxiety, hallucinations, and memory loss listed in the side effects. They are listed in the "unlikely but serious side effects that you should inform your doctor of right away" part of the information sheet that I threw away without reading.

Since he hadn't been hearing voices before he started taking medication, he probably should have been taken off that prescription, and put on some other anti-depressant. That is why it is important to read your medicine documentation, and don't hesitate to raise concerns about side effects you are experiencing. Some side effects are rare, so your doctor may not think of the medication as the problem, even if it is.

Getting Through Middle School

It had been decided at Joey's old school, that it would be best if he rode the special education bus. There were less kids on that bus, and the children on that bus were more accepting because they had disabilities of their own. The solution had worked well for Joey. However, when we moved to Don's town, Joey's new teacher, Mrs. B. insisted there was nothing wrong with Joey, and he didn't need that bus. What's more, Mrs. B. also questioned if he was really autistic. Her fellow teacher had an autistic son, and she'd met him. Mrs. B. said that boy was nothing like Joey, which proved Joey was probably just faking it to get attention.

Joey loved his new teacher, but that woman stood on my last nerve, and I had to fight Mrs. B. tooth and nail for every accommodation Joey ever got. Finally, Mrs. B. insisted that Joey's psychiatrist be invited to his I. E. P. because she wanted his opinion whether Joey really needed the special education bus. His doctor's office was in a neighboring town, and Joey's psychiatrist refused to meet in person. However, he agreed that if they would pay for an hour of his time, we could have a conference call in the principal's office.

We all crowded around the principal's desk, and he put Joey's Doctor on the speaker phone. After the meeting was called to order, and we went around the room telling the doctor who all was in attendance, Mrs. B. began her regular speech about how nothing was wrong with Joey, and accommodations should stop being made.

I remember the doctor cut her off mid-sentence. He told Mrs. B. the reason she wasn't seeing any behaviors in Joey was that he had Joey on six very strong psychotic medications. Each had side effect warnings an arms width long. The doctor said Joey needed all those drugs, just to be able to enter their school building! Instead of discussing removing accommodations, they needed to do their job and make Joey's life more comfortable, so he could take Joey off some of those drugs before they caused permanent damage. You could have heard a pin drop in that room!

No one at that school ever talked about taking accommodations away from Joey again. The next year, they put Joey in the class with the teacher who had the autistic son. That teacher told me she was so grateful to get to teach Joey, because she saw many similarities in Joey and her son's behaviors. Her son was non-verbal, so she couldn't ask him why he did the things he did, but Joey could explain his reasoning's, and it helped her understand her own son more.

The year after, Joey was supposed to move up to High School. He should have gone to the High School Michael was going to, but I didn't want him to go there. Michael was having a hard enough time getting the accommodations that he needed, and Michael was my compliant child. I knew things would be much more stressful for Joey.

The inner city high school had an autism program, and I wanted Joey to go there because I thought Joey would get teachers who were better equipped to meet his needs. When I went to the I. E. P. and requested the change in schools, the principal of Michael's school, was the husband of Joey's teacher, and the father of that nonverbal autistic child. After stating all the reasons I wanted Joey moved to the autism program at the inner city school, the principal told me the autism program would be more expensive, and his school would have to pay for it.

He said it was their policy that no student was allowed to go to the other school's autism program, unless they first failed at their school. I broke into tears and said I couldn't afford for Joey to fail to thrive at another school. I wasn't sure he'd live through the experience. So in light of Joey's past suicide attempts, they made an exception for Joey, and let him go straight to the Autism program at the inner city high school.

Joey's I. E. P. (Individualized Educational Plan) at the high school read that he would be main streamed with the other kids, but he would get a hall pass and extra time between classes so he could avoid the crowded halls. He was also allowed a safe spot in the Special Education room where he could go if his anxiety kicked up. He would be allowed to stay there and do his homework until his anxieties relieved enough that he could go back to class. He got to continue to ride the Special Education bus.

After a couple weeks in his first year at high school, Joey came home from school very upset. I asked him what was wrong, and he said his Special Ed. teacher talked about him to another teacher in front of him and another boy. She was asking her advice on how to handle Joey, and Joey was embarrassed and upset.

I was furious and went straight to the principal to discuss it. I was afraid my feelings were too raw. If I tried talking directly to the teacher, I might end up yelling at Ms. C. or crying, myself. I thought the principal was just the level head and buffer we needed. What I didn't know, was it was Ms. C's first year teaching autistic kids, and her first year at that school. What's worse, the teacher she was talking to was actually her faculty advisor who was training her in this job.

Had I talked to her first, she could have explained that, and I'd have probably been way less angry. But I still think she messed up by talking about my son in front of him and another boy. She justified it by saying it was okay, because the other boy was non-verbal and wouldn't repeat it to anyone, anyway, but even if a child is non-verbal, that doesn't mean they can't listen and understand, and it could affect his opinion of Joey. They were peers after all.

I think training sessions should happen out of ear shot of students, but I really should have talked to her before going to her boss with the problem. I apologized at the first parent teacher conference, when Ms. C. brought up the subject and explained her side. But it wasn't long before Ms. C. got the opportunity to prove just how invaluable she really was.

Chapter 19

The Pool and the Beanbag Chair

One of the things Joey was excited about at that high school was it had a huge swimming pool in the basement. Joey was a little fish. He was thrilled to take swimming for his P. E. class. About that time, Joey met his friend, Chris, and they took swimming together. Chris also liked to swim. One day, they got to playing in the deep end of the pool, and Joey dunked Chris. It must have alarmed the P. E. teacher, because she blew her whistle and said for Joey to get out of the pool. Joey didn't hear what she said, so he swam over to her life guard chair, and asked what she needed. She repeated the command to get out of the pool.

Joey asked, "Why should I? I haven't done anything wrong."

"Yes, you did!" She replied. "You tried to drown that other student."

"No, I didn't!" He retorted.

"You most certainly did!" She answered. "I saw you dunk Chris, and that's dangerous! You could have killed him!"

"I dunked Chris." Joey replied. "But that's not dangerous. My Dad used to dunk me when we were playing around, and my Dad would never try to kill me."

With that, he casually swam back over to the other side of the pool, and lowered himself in the water just low enough that only the top half of his head with his nose was above water. She called for the principal, and he tried to get Joey to leave, but since Joey was convinced he'd done nothing wrong, he refused to obey him as well. The principal made all the other kids leave the pool, shut off the heater and turned out the lights, and still Joey wouldn't get out. Finally, not knowing what else to do, the principal called for the special education teacher Ms. C. to come to the gym.

Ms. C. came over, and asked Joey what was wrong. Joey told her the PE teacher was picking on him, because she accused him of trying to kill his friend when he was only playing with him. She sympathized with Joey, but also told him the principal had decided to suspend him for three days since Joey wasn't respecting authority. "Do you want to come hang out in my room and read a book on my beanbag chair until your Mom comes? " She asked him. Joey loved reading and found the bean bag chair in the corner of her room very comfortable.

"Sure!" He said, and jumped out of the pool, toweled off and followed Ms. C. to her room. The principal was amazed she handled it so well, and told me himself when he called me to his office to tell me his side of the story, and ask me to take my son home for his suspension. Chris apologized to Ms. C. for getting Joey in trouble.

Ms. C thought it was sweet of Chris to apologize, and told me. I called Chris' mom, Janet, to tell her thanks, for her son sticking up for Joey. After that, we scheduled a play date between the boys and they became best friends

Joey continued to be like a fish out of water in that school. He was miserable from the minute he entered the building. He had a safe spot in Ms. C's room. It was in his I. E. P. that anytime life got too stressful, he was allowed to leave and go to Ms. C's room. He'd hang out on her bean bag chair until he felt ready to go back to class.

Unfortunately, Joey was never ready to go back to class. He was happy as a lark, hanging out on Ms. C's bean bag chair reading books. He even convinced the other students it was his spot, and if Joey came in and found someone else sitting there, he'd evict them so he could have his spot back. It irritated Ms. C. though, and eventually she told me so.

One day during her planning meeting, Ms. C. called me. "Your son is not getting an education. I thought you should know that. Joey's taking full advantage of the Safe Spot in his I. E. P. and spending from the time he gets to school until the time he goes home, hanging out on my bean bag chair, reading books from the library. So I guess if you just want my free babysitting and to avoid truancy issues, you're good, but if you care about Joey's future and want him to get an education, I thought you should know: he's not getting one."

I made an appointment with Joey's Psychiatrist, and he wrote on a prescription pad that Joey needed to be home-bound for anxiety reasons. At first, the school was a little mad about that. They didn't think his doctor should be able to prescribe a more expensive form of education, and force the school system to pay for it. But in the end, they couldn't find a way to avoid it. From then on, I'd drive Joey to meet with Ms. C. at a burger joint and later a taco place on Tuesday mornings. She'd gather up all the teacher's weekly assignments and explain them to Joey. Then Ms. C. would meet us again on Friday to collect all his homework, and give it to the teachers to grade.

He kept that up until the last semester of his senior year. Then, the principal said he had to attend school there to get a regular diploma. Even then, he was allowed to do all his work in the safety of Ms. C.'s room. She had become such an ally, that she even helped plan and decorate for Joey's Senior open house. You could say Ms. C. had quite a vested interest. Joey graduated with honors. He worked hard to earn those grades, but I don't think he could have done it without Ms. C.'s help. I am so grateful that she called and let me know Joey wasn't being educated, and something needed to change!

Chapter 20

A More Proactive Approach

When Joey turned 18 he quit all of his medication abruptly, he'd hated taking it for years, but since I and his psychiatrist thought he needed it, he'd humored us both until he was eighteen. Then he said, "Legally you can't make me take that, and I'm done with it." I was really concerned what would happen to him without the medication, but it turned out not to be an issue. I guess he didn't really need any drugs now that we'd made the accommodation he'd needed at school…

Both Michael and Joey graduated from High school, Michael in 2009, and Joey in 2010. They both enrolled at a local community college only to drop out less than a year later calling it a waste of time and money. Joey in particular was quite vocal on the issue saying:

> "They wouldn't even let me take the classes I wanted because they had 'prerequisites'. They forced me to pay them like a thousand dollars so that they could waste my time reteaching me basic algebra even though I aced the math section of the SAT. I didn't do any of the homework and I still passed that class it was that easy. There isn't anything I can learn here that I couldn't learn faster for free on the internet, and the diploma isn't worth the time and monetary cost."

Then a whole lot of nothing happened. Joey really struggled to find a job, it took Joey four years to land a Quality Assurance Tester job working from home at a relatively new company. Then one day, the house next door came up for sale. It seemed perfect, Joey, and Michael could move right next door. That would give them a bit more independence and they could come over anytime by just walking. Joey used his whole live savings (which was basically a couple years pay) and Don cashed out a large chunk of his 401K and together they bought the house and the boys moved next door.

Whenever you change your living arrangements, what affects one effects all. Since Don and I are so much older than our son, Jeromy (I was forty-two when he was born), and he was extremely active since birth, the boys always played an instrumental part in raising him. Whether they were playing with Jeromy, or stopping him from doing something unsafe, they could keep up with him when I could not.

My three sons had a very special bond, and Jeromy relied on Michael and Joey's wit and wisdom to get him through his days. Jeromy was not happy to have his brothers even move next door, but we convinced him it was okay. They still came home for nearly every meal, and Jeromy was allowed to go visit them as often as he wanted. Before long, the boys had worn a path between our two houses, and for a brief while, the situation felt ideal.

That changed suddenly when shortly after the boys moved next door, Don's parents passed away within six months of each other. They left us the family home his Dad built. It was his parents' desire for us to live in it and keep it in the family. We moved a forty-five minute drive away from the boys. After that, we went from seeing Michael and Joey multiple times a day, and having most meals in common to only seeing them a couple times a week. Jeromy resented moving, and having to leave his friends. He was lonely without his brothers, and angry at us for moving him without giving him a choice.

Jeromy got mad and resentful, and soon he was throwing the same kind of fits Joey used to throw, but with much different outcomes. This time, I had Michael and Joey to consult with me on how to handle the situation. I also took a short course on nonviolent communication. Unlike when I was raising my other two, I was mature enough now to not care what others thought. I wanted what was best for Jeromy, and I was pretty sure that included avoiding unnecessary medication, and criminal records. When Jeromy refused to go to school, I remembered all the struggles Joey had trying to fit into new schools, and agreed to home school him instead.

Still, Jeromy really missed his brothers and his old life. Jeromy's angry outbursts were getting more frequent. Jeromy was miserable without his brothers, and finally started making threats that he would kill himself. As soon as Joey heard that, he said, "Michael and I are moving back in. We are not willing to lose Jeromy to suicide!"

I said, "I don't think he really means it. I think Jeromy is just saying it to get attention."

Joey said, "I never meant it either. I threatened because I wanted attention, and then when no one believed me, I had to try so people would take me seriously. Over twenty times I made halfhearted attempts to take my life, all the while hoping I wouldn't succeed, but it would be enough to get your attention so I could get help with the underlying conditions that made me so miserable. If Jeromy's threatening suicide, I'm moving home! I'll give up my own life as I know it, to let Jeromy know I value his."

I was shocked to learn that Joey had attempted suicide over twenty times. I'd say most of those attempts went unnoticed. I thought it had been less than ten. I'm so glad he never went through with it, because he's grown up to be such a loving, loyal, intelligent, witty, fun friend and son. I can't imagine life without him in it.

Chapter 21

Where are we now?

    This afternoon, Don, Michael, Joey, Jeromy and I piled into our SUV and drove to the bookstore. It was that same store where I made my promise to God all those years ago, and we all like to go back there once a month or so because it still is the best bookstore anywhere near us even if it is more than an hour drive. How fitting that my story of our life should circle back to the place where it started! Life is a kind of like that, isn't it? One big circle, I mean.

    I have to say, this trip was much more pleasant then the one at the beginning of my book. Instead of being alone, I had my family with me, and truth be told, I didn't really even look for a book today. I sipped coffee with Don in the cafe, while the boys looked over all the books together.

Then, instead of me going to my car, crying my eyes out and making God promises if He'd save my family, we piled into our car together, drove to one of our favorite nearby restaurants, and ordered a delicious dinner. Don prayed for our meal and we thanked God for each other and our many blessings, and drove home together thankful for such a fun evening as a family.

It's been a couple years since the boys moved back in with us now. Jeromy calmed back down, and is no longer violent, running away, or threatening to kill himself. This time around we didn't resort to medicine. If Jeromy said anything about wanting to die he wasn't allowed to be alone again until he calmed down, and when Jeromy took off running out the door we'd just throw on a coat and take off after him. We'd follow behind him quietly as he stomped down the street until he had time to cool off. Then he'd slow down and let us catch up, and what started out as a run-a-way attempt turned into a walk with friends. If Jeromy got violent, Joey would give him a hug and just let Jeromy beat against his back and scratch at his arms until he was tired, and calm enough to talk things out. When Jeromy would scream in his face, "I hate you" Joey always replied back, "But I love you".

Around the same time, Jeromy and I found a wonderful Christian Counselor to see. She talked with us, and helped us work through the problems that were bothering Jeromy. By seeking help early, we only needed a little direction to work out our issues on our own, instead of letting it blow up into a medical issue like we did with Joey. It took about a year to help Jeromy work through his trauma, but now Jeromy's back to being a happy kid which was totally worth the effort.

I try to spend a lot of time with my kids. We go for walks, play board games, and I've even learned to play a few video games with the boys, they aren't really my thing, but it means a lot to Jeromy that I'm willing to care about the things he cares about. Even though I'm not really that good at video games, it doesn't really matter. Jeromy just appreciates the fact I'm spending time with him doing what he loves. Seeing Jeromy happy makes it more enjoyable to me, too. I'm still home-schooling Jeromy, which considering how rough 2020 was for normal schools turned out to be a huge blessing.

Jeromy is still much too hyper to sit still for a whole class like in regular school. Often Jeromy paces while I ask him his questions and scribe for him, but Jeromy gets his work done. In traditional schools he was sent out of the room if Jeromy couldn't sit still, and that made him feel like he was being bad or was inferior to others. Don also brings Jeromy along with him sometimes when Don does drain cleaning or plumbing jobs. It gives them special bonding time alone, and teaches Jeromy valuable skills of a trade, in case Jeromy chooses to follow in his Dad's footsteps, and take over the company when he is older.

If your kids have special needs, I'd say the most important thing to teach them is that God created them that way for a reason, and they should embrace who they are instead of letting society shame them for it. If you can teach your children that they are valuable, loved and were created by God for a purpose, as long as you've taught them the basics of reading, math, how to study, and how to pray, I believe eventually they will find their way.

Joey had to retire because of medical reasons. His anxiety issues and his narcolepsy, made it too hard to keep up with the demands of QA work as the company grew and the industry started to shift more towards "agile development", whatever that is. Joey started having panic attacks, and then ultimately retired onto disability.

Michael's obsessive compulsive disorder, and his perfectionist attitude often trip him up from completing the things he wants to do. The boys' autism and other disorders do put them at a terrible disadvantage, and for now, both my older boys are on social security and renting a room in our house, but they are as independent as they can be. They are currently working on making a video game. However, they keep changing their mind about what it is they want to make so it is slow going.

As you can see, we aren't a perfect family. We still have our struggles and we still have lots of things we are working on improving or figuring out, but we love each other and we enjoy simple things together like playing board games, going for walks, talking about all sorts of interesting things we've been reading about, having Pizza parties, and "Make your own Tacos night".

We experience our share of disappointments, power struggles and general chaos, but through it all we pray with and for each other. We know whatever we are facing today isn't out of God's control. He's got this! We just have to trust and wait and see how it all works out, and knowing that is called faith. Faith in God's ability to see our family through whatever comes our way is what gives us peace and joy. That's what I pray God gives your family too.

Lessons Learned

The book I promised God that I would write was one that would tell a Mom how to help her teenage son overcome his suicidal thoughts and live. That was the type of book I was looking for that day, but honestly, we're nearing the end of this book, and I'm trying to prepare you to go on without me. Frankly, imparting sound advice seems more important than making sure my book flows in a smooth chronological order. That is why these chapters highlight some of the lessons I've learned along the way.

These lessons are far from an exhaustive list of things that can be learned from what we went through, but I feel that they are some of the more important things I picked up and I wanted to be sure to pass them on.

Chapter 22

A Willingness to Listen is Powerful

Writing this book proved more difficult than I thought it would be. The reason I had such a hard time writing this book is that I witnessed my miracle without understanding it. I didn't have the answers, I jumped to conclusions, over reacted, and brought a bazooka to a water gun fight, so to speak. Instead of being there for Joey when he needed me, I assembled my team of highly esteemed professionals who were going to "Fix Joey". As long as it was me against him, the problem intensified. He felt isolated, and the more we pushed him under the microscope, and all of us stood back and observed his every move, the more the problem got worse.

The life sustaining moments weren't the ones where we tried to analyze Joey, and fix his problems. They were the moments we both let our guard down, and accepted each other as we were and just enjoyed time together.

No matter how frustrating life is right now, how much you hate the choices your loved one is making. Ask them to go do something fun with you. We were broke in those days, so fun for us consisted of nightly walks where we could talk about our day. It is important not to be judgmental if you want them to open up to you. If you rebuke them when they confide in you, they will be less likely to do so in the future. Even if the things they have to say are alarming it is better that they are said to a friend than pondered alone.

I learned this from a friend of mine. Shelly had a troubled life growing up, and those feelings followed her into adulthood. Shelly struggled with depression and thoughts of suicide. She had the scars to prove it. On one wrist Shelly had two scars, and on the other she had one, where three times Shelly had slit her wrist. She and I also used to go for walks, and it seemed more often than not, in a joking manner Shelly would say her day was going so bad she might as well kill herself.

I found that very troubling, and eventually asked her to stop saying that, and I'll never forget her response. Shelly said, "Oh, Cyndi, please don't ever make me stop talking about suicide! It's a feeling that haunts me most of the time. When people let me talk about it, the feeling subsides, but when I hold it in, it festers and grows. As long as I'm joking about it, I'm not doing it. But when I quit joking about it, that's when you need to worry!"

Shelly held out her arms with her hands palms up, and exposed her scars to me. "I never talked to anyone about my feelings before I did these cuts. They just happened to find me in a pool of my own blood. I didn't want to tell anyone, because I didn't want to be saved. Don't refuse to talk to people who have suicidal feelings, because as long as they are talking, they aren't doing." Shelly's words were a precious gift to me, because they were a reminder, we're all in this together. God never meant for us to go it alone. You don't have to know the answers to help someone, sometimes all they need is someone willing to listen.

Clear back in the Garden of Eden, when God first made man, *"Then the Lord God said, 'It is not good that the man should be alone. I will make him a helper suitable for him.'" -Genesis 2:18* This was right after God had created man because He wanted us for a relationship with Him. God could have easily said, "I'll be enough for him. I will fulfill his every need." But God didn't! He said, *"It's not good for man to be alone."*

The Bible also says, *"And if someone might overpower another by himself, two together can withstand him. A threefold cord is not quickly broken." -Ecclesiastes 4:12* God wants us to be there for each other. Loneliness and suicide seem to go hand in hand. It's important to keep the social connections we have and continue to make more as we go along. Reach out to your loved ones in friendship and encourage them to get involved in a church youth group, sports, and/or any other activities that they would enjoy that would also help them to make more friends. The more positive connections they have in their lives, the less opportunities those negative feelings will have to take a deadly grip on them.

Chapter 23

Avoid Tunnel Vision & Assess Your Options

The thing I liked best about my job at the yellow page company was I had a half hour commute from the time I dropped Michael off at school until I pulled into work, and an hour long drive home. That gave me time to switch gears from one difficult job to the other. The phone book job had a nice benefits package with health insurance and sick days, but that was about all it had going for it... Unless you count the free coffee in the break-room. Everyday, I packed a peanut butter sandwich and an apple in my purse, and after dropping off the boys at school, I headed to my own little version of Hell on Earth.

We were paid strictly on commission, and after the eighteen revenue accounts they gave me ran dry, I was responsible for getting my own leads. I had to keep all the Revenue accounts that I was assigned in the book, plus increase the book's sales by thirty percent, before I could move on to the next market. If anyone defaulted on their payments over the course of the year, I had to go collect their late payment, or be charged back for the commission I'd earned on their sale. Also, as soon as they started selling a new Market, the managers could start giving away your accounts from the previous campaign to new employees.

I lost a lot of my good customers because the managers took them from me when I was stuck in an unprofitable market, because I was having a difficult time growing that book by thirty percent. I knew the exact dollar amount I had to earn weekly to be able to pay my monthly bills. Those were my weekly goals, and I couldn't stop working until I reached my quota. It was a struggle to make ends meet, and often I took work home. I'd be prospecting leads over the phone on weekends to try to fill my calendar with appointments for the next week.

Looking back, one of the worst things about that time was I had complete tunnel vision. I was so hyper focused on working to provide for my kids that I was working to the point of exhaustion and had little energy left to parent. My boys had to raise themselves. They had to try to navigate the waters of being the new kid in Middle school alone. Those were very choppy waters and they didn't have anyone, parent or otherwise, to turn to for advice.

If I could have stepped back and looked at the problem objectively, I was a displaced homemaker at that point. I bet I could have applied for food stamps, welfare, and gotten grants to go back to school to learn a good trade. The kids and I could have been sitting around the dinner table together doing our homework, and in a few short years, I'd have been able to get a well paying job where I didn't have to spend so much time away from my boys when they needed me most!

I've realized that by trying my hardest and staying the course, no matter what, I hurt my kids more than anyone else did. I'd advise you to take a step back, bring a notebook, and go off by yourself to a park, or some other breath taking slice of nature. Pray to God to give you wisdom, and direct your steps. Then, really think about all the different options available to you.

When you lift your nose from the grindstone and consider the future as well as today, you can find little blocks of time to spend together with the people you love. You might try starting the habit of doing paperwork together at the table after supper.

If you aren't already, I recommend eating dinner together at the table with the TV off, and electronics put away. It doesn't matter if the food is home cooked or not, or even if it's healthy for that matter. The important thing is to sit around the table and discuss each other's day in a positive way. Start off with each of you sharing one thing you liked about the day. It can be anything really. You are showing them that you love them, you care about what they are going through, and they are worthy of your time.

Be prepared to share first, and don't pressure them if they can't think of anything the first few days. Just keep sharing your stories, and eventually, perhaps they'll open up and share too. Most importantly, you need to be accepting. Be careful how you react to what they share. You want them to feel like this is a safe place to bring their problems. Don't judge them or correct them for what they choose to share. Let them know that if they ever have a problem, they can turn to you for help, and you'll be on their side, not against them.

Chapter 24

Reaching for the Lifeline

One night back when we were still living in the trailer and Joey was getting the cops called every week, Mary, our in-home counselor, the one you get after you've flunked out of the meet me at my office kind of counselor, had slipped me a paper with a phone number on it as she left my house a few hours before. She'd said, "Here. I want you to give this number a call. She's agreed to take your call. I think she can really help you. She was where you are just a few years ago. I helped her through it, and we'll get you through it too. Give her a call. Maybe she has some practical advice you can use."

I put that folded up paper in the pocket of my pants, and got started making dinner. Every so often, I reached in my pocket to feel it still there. It gave me a little spark of hope each time I poked my finger on it's folded corner. I could hardly wait, but I had to wait, because it was too important of a call to mess up. I finished getting supper ready, and called the boys to the table to eat.

We ate our supper, finished up homework, did the dishes, watched a little TV, read their bedtime story, and said their prayers. I turned out the light and walked out of their room. I could hardly suppress my excitement as I read a little while, making sure they had time to fall asleep. Then I fixed myself a cup of coffee and walked out onto the front porch with my phone and the folded paper in hand.

Have you seen that old game show where people answer multiple choice questions for a chance to win a million dollars? In the show, a contestant tries to answer a series of questions without ever answering any wrong in hopes of winning a million dollars. They get three lifelines for when they get stuck on a question. One lifeline is called 50/50, where you get the show to remove the two most obviously wrong choices to increase your odds of choosing the right answer, another they get to poll the audience and see which choice they would choose before making their decision, and the best life line is they can call a friend. Right there, during the biggest crisis moment of the show, they can say, "I'd like to call a friend." The show gets their friend on the phone, and the contestant can ask their advice on how to answer the question. They choose their wisest friend, preferably someone who's got a little experience with this type of question. I'm sure it's such a relief to be able to count on that friend to help them solve the problem, right when they need it most. That's how I felt that night.

God and I spent many a tearful night out there under the stars. Usually I'd be begging Him for wisdom, direction or just to take all the painful struggles away, but tonight was different! Tonight, I had a lifeline. There would be a real voice on the other end of the phone, and my counselor believed this person could really help me! I was filled with nervous excitement as I dialed the number and listened to it ring.

"Hello?"

"Hi. I'm Cyndi. I hope I'm not calling too late, but I had to get my kids to bed first. I got your number from my counselor, Mary. She thought maybe you'd be able to help me. Give me some advice about how to handle my suicidal son. I hope it's okay I called."

"Yes, I told Mary I'd take your call. I owe her one. She helped us a couple of years ago when we were in a similar situation. I'd say, she saved my son's life. She thinks it will help if I talk to you, so this is how this is going to work. You get one call. I owe Mary that much. This is it. I'll answer any question you ask, and stay on the line as long as you need tonight, but after we hang up, you can throw my number away, because I've got yours on caller ID, and I'll never take another call from you again. Do we have an agreement?"

Wow! I felt like she'd just sucker punched me in the gut! My mind was reeling. Why was she being like this? It seemed like the nicest and most horrible thing all rolled into one. I'd have liked to argue or tell her she was being unfair, but I couldn't. She might have information that I needed to save my son. I had to be grateful for the crumbs she offered, and try to clear my head enough to ask all the pertinent questions I'd need to know now and in the future.

It was a crazy phone call. I wish I'd known what to expect in advance. I'd have spent hours writing questions before making that call. That's what made it feel so much like the game show's life line. There was no time to prepare, and everything was on the line! I didn't care about being a millionaire. I had a much more valuable prize at stake! I needed to know how to save my son from the suicidal thoughts that plagued him and threatened to steal him away from me.

I don't even remember the questions I asked. Through the course of the conversation, I learned her son was autistic and in his early twenties. He lived at home and probably always will. Her son had also struggled with suicidal thoughts. He wasn't currently suicidal, but something tells me it wasn't too far in the past, because his mom seemed to fear those thoughts could resurface at any time. I think that might be why I was limited to one phone call. Maybe hearing about my son made her fear that her son would revert back to those days.

Through the course of the conversation, she let it slip that she lived in the same trailer park I lived in. She'd seen us going for our nightly walks, and knew who I was, but I had no idea where she lived and who she and her son were. Maybe that was why she didn't want a long term friendship with me. Perhaps she saw the frequency that police cars were in our driveway and she feared my son might harm my friends too, or teach her son bad behaviors. I'm sure she felt she had good reasons, but it kind of creep-ed me out each time I looked at my neighbors after that. I'd wonder, "Are you the one I bared my soul to that night?"

It seemed to me like she should have allowed me to be her friend. It seems like I could have encouraged her through rough days, and she could have done the same for me. But for whatever reason, she felt the scales were unfairly tipped in my favor. She had more to lose than she had to gain, so the relationship would end at the end of the phone call. Ironically, the thing I learned most from that call was what was not said. "No man is an island." When life is tough, it's tempting to gather your little chicks under your wings and shelter them from the world, but I don't believe this is what you should do. If you do, you isolate them and yourself.

You can't get help when you refuse to reach out. You can't grow, when you shelter yourself in your home, block out the windows and avoid people. Your life stagnates and the more stagnant it gets the less appealing it is. Reach out! Spend time with others. Share, even when it feels like an unfair trade. Make connections! I believe God created us to be in community with each other. Jesus said:

> "A new commandment I give to you, that you love one another, even as I have loved you, that you also love one another." -John 13:34 MEV

I spent over an hour on that call, grilling her about everything I could imagine that my boys might experience between their age and her son's age. After I couldn't think of a single thing more to ask, I still hesitated to hang up, because I was afraid I'd think of something else to ask later.

The finality of the call kind of reminded me of death. After that call, I would be dead to her. I really couldn't understand how a person can shut people off like that. Know all about their problems, but just refuse to care. I think it happens gradually. Either you open up to others, or you close yourself off. It starts out innocently enough. "I can't have anyone over! What would they think of my messy house?" or "I've got enough problems of my own right now. I can't worry about theirs too!" Decision after decision, day after day, throughout your life, you get to choose to turn inward to self or outward to others. The healthy choice is to reach out. Each time you help someone else with something they are going through, you are creating a special bond. All those connections will see you through the next time life sucker punches you in the gut.

Sheltering your loved ones from the harshness of life will stagnate their growth the same way it stagnates your own. So encourage them to try things on their own, and remind them if they need you, you are only a phone call away, and they'll never need to lose your number, because you will always take their call.

My little sister, Tracey, and her family live about an hour away from us. We don't get together as often as we'd like, but at least a couple times a week we call to catch up on each other's news. As we go to hang up, Tracey always says, "You pray for our family and I'll pray for yours." I love that! That's the kind of lifeline you can really use! Someone who will keep you in their prayers and in their heart, and give you an invitation to "Call anytime you need to talk." Those are the kind of people who really make a difference. That's the kind of person I want to be too.

I can't publish my real name or my contact information in this book and say call me whenever, because honestly if even a dozen people took me up on that I could very well never have free time again, and I won't live forever so when I'm gone it would be fairly pointless. Also, as much as I want to help you better understand your suicidal child, I also want my three boys to be able to leave that dark chapter in their past without having the entire world know them for it. I want a bright future for your kids and mine. That said I don't want to leave you empty handed so here are a couple of phone numbers that are a bit more likely to be of help to you.

At the time of writing:

The National Alliance on Mental Illness or NAMI offers a free nation wide peer-support service called the NAMI HelpLine that can be reached Monday through Friday 10AM-8PM Eastern Time at:

    1-800-950-NAMI

    That's **1-800-950-6264** if you prefer your phone numbers to be just numbers.

    If phone calls aren't your thing (Michael and Joey both hate making calls so I understand this can be an issue) the **NAMI HelpLine also has an email address: info@nami.org**

For free 24/7 support there is the National Suicide Prevention Lifeline which can be reached at:

    1-800-273-TALK

    1-800-273-8255 if you prefer the numbers to the letters.

If you have a crisis you can reach the Crisis Text Line 24/7 for free by texting HOME to 741741 but there are a few things to be aware of:

1. **Their system has a 160 character limit on the messages** so you will likely need to send a bunch of short messages, rather than the wall of text you might prefer.

2. While the **Crisis Text Line does not charge texters, the same might not be true for your phone provider**. At time of writing if your phone plan is from **AT&T, T-Mobile, Sprint, or Verizon texts to the short code 741741 are free of charge**. Otherwise assume your standard text message rate applies.

3. **Shortcodes like 741741 are not universally supported**, notably they are not allowed on many prepaid plans **if your phone can't reach the Crisis Text Line via text they are also available via Facebook Messenger at: facebook.com/crisistextline**

4. **The Crisis Text Line has stated that their goal is to respond to every texter in under five minutes, but that may not always be possible** and wait times may vary depending on how many texts they are receiving.

Hopefully one of the above contacts may be of use to you if you need them, I personally would have liked to have known about them at the time.

Chapter 25

On Parenting

Sometimes I think playing it safe might be one of the most dangerous games there is. I grew up Catholic, and we didn't believe in divorce. My Dad was always the head of our family, and I expected no less from the man I married! I falsely believed when the bible said, *"Wives, be submissive to your own husbands as unto the Lord." — Ephesians 5:22 MEV* that meant that if I let him make all the choices, all the mistakes would be his too, and I could waltz into Heaven unscathed no matter what we did.

I was in effect trying to use Mike as my own personal fall guy. If he told me to sin, and I sinned, then he'd get in trouble, not me. I was just obeying like the Bible said, but that's just not how life works. I could just have easily quoted the story of Ananias and Sapphira in *Acts 5:1-11*, where the couple sold their property to give the money to the Church, but conspired to lie and say they gave it all when really they held some back. God struck them both dead.

It's important to note that although the Bible says to submit to your husband, "As unto the Lord" it doesn't say instead of to the Lord. Accept no substitutes, ask God to direct your footsteps, give you wisdom, and show you how best to raise your family.

Honestly though, I didn't believe I could take care of myself, so I jumped at the chance the first time a guy offered to sweep me off my feet. Who knows if another offer would come along. A bird in the hand is worth two in the bush, right? I might be being a little hard on myself. I honestly thought I was in love, but looking back, I was probably more in love with the thought of being in love. We were nothing alike from the beginning.

I wish I could say that I've always modeled unconditional love to my kids. The truth is, when I first had my kids, I was immature and cared more about the appearance of our family life than the true condition of it. I think my ex-husband and I saw our kids as little miniature trophies instead of individuals to love and nurture on their own paths. I naively thought babies were my little do-it yourself project that I could shape into anything I wanted. My son's pediatrician said there is a time table when kids are supposed to learn certain things. I felt personally responsible for making sure they hit all the milestones everyone expects of their child from the day they are born.

I wanted them to do well in school, have friends and a girl friend, play sports, be in school clubs, get a driver's license, get a job, graduate with honors and scholarships, do well in College, get a lucrative career, each of them find a perfect wife, have children and be involved in their kid's lives, let me babysit and be the perfect Grandma, take their families on fun vacations and see the world, they should also be good Christian roll models for their children, save for retirement, live a full life, retire, and eventually die a peaceful death leaving the world a better place than the way they found it.

No pressure, right? It's laughable when I see that list written out, but it seemed perfectly reasonable at the time.

Since the hospital didn't provide me with a handbook of how to train a child when they released me to bring my little bundles home, I just kinda winged it. Basing my parenting style loosely on how I was raised, along with stuff I read in parenting magazines and advise from other Mom's I knew. One thing I've noticed after a lifetime of parenting, it's always easier to know how to raise someone else kids, than the ones God gave you. I might be pulling my hair out trying to figure out how to help my boy with a problem he's going through, but see a kid at the park bullying another child, and I have to suppress the urge to tell the Mom, "If he were my boy, I'd...". It took me years to realize that.

I'm ashamed to admit many times my parental intervention and reprimands were more based on what the neighbors would think than what I genuinely felt was best for my child. We raised my first two boys at the beginning of the "Spankings are cruel" era, but they didn't give us advise as to what would really work instead. Time outs seemed to be the approved method, but seemed ineffective to us. If that was the worst you would do, what would motivate them to stay in time out? People joked about using duct tape, but you weren't really allowed to.

I hate to admit it, but I found shame to be a highly effective tool to keep them planted in their time-out seat. At the time I thought I was really on to something! I'd even brag to friends that "I don't ever have to spank Michael. All I have to do is look him in the eye and tell him sternly, 'I am very disappointed in you!' and he'll jump through hoops to change his behavior in order to please me." I thought I'd found a lesser punishment that worked.

When Joey was going through his tough times, Community Mental Health sent me to a parenting class. I passed the class with flying colors and got my diploma to prove it, but it didn't help our situation one bit. Basically, they told me to make a list of things I'd like done, so my kids could make restitution when they did something wrong, anything from household chores, to playing a board game with me, drawing me a bubble bath, or entertaining themselves an hour to give me some much deserved time alone.

It sounded great to me! I whipped up that list in no time. I also made a list of Family Rules and posted them for all to see. The first time Joey messed up, I told him, "When you yell at me, it drain's Mom's energy. On the fridge is a list of things that will help get Mom's energy back. Since you drained my energy, go pick what you want to do to give me my energy back."

He took a look at that list, and said, "Oh no you don't! You are responsible for taking care of yourself! Just because I screwed up, doesn't give you the right to pawn your chores off on me!"

He crumpled the list and threw it in the trash. I never bothered to print another one. I went out to the porch and thought about it. He was right. If we teach our kids their place in our family is conditional to their good behavior, how do they ever feel cherished or secure?

One of my kid's counselors told me that often the reason a child tries to break the rules is they want to know how strong the rule is. Well devised strong rules can provide safety and prove that you care, but bad rules are oppressive. You have to ask yourself, "Why does this rule exist in the first place? Is it for my child's benefit or my personal comfort?"

When I look back at my older sons' early lives, my ex-husband and I were immature and most of our rules were more about impressing others with what good parents we were and how our little ones could toe the line, than about preparing our kids for a successful adulthood. Those rules really needed to go! If after careful contemplation, you are sure this rule is in your child's best interest, then explain to your child why the rule exists in the first place, and then hold fast to your rule in a loving way.

If we are to model God's love, how do they learn to trust God if we give them lists of demands that they have to meet if they want to earn our favor? If our human families are supposed to be a reflection of God's heavenly one, and we as parents are supposed to train up our children in the way they should go, shouldn't we be modeling hope and grace too, so our kids will want to look for God because we've shown them a glimpse of His goodness? I decided to love and pray more, and try to lecture and punish less.

When we use language like, "As long as you live under my roof, you will obey me!", we raise little bullies who think the biggest and the toughest make the rules. That's not how God taught us to live, but if were aren't going to punish, then what is the answer?

One thing I did, and I'd advise you to do as well, was when Joey was being his most defiant, after he fell asleep, I'd go stand in his doorway and watch him sleep a few minutes. There in the quiet of his room, he looked sweet and innocent as he slept, and it reminded me of the sweet little baby that I knew and loved. Moments like that reminded me that although we were going through a tough time, the sweet little boy I knew and loved was still in there, and this too would pass. We'd get through this eventually and come out closer on the other side for having gone through it together.

Instead of automatically parenting the way you were parented, or letting someone else tell you how to raise your kids, I recommend reverse engineering the process. Think about how you want your kids to turn out. Do you want them to be independent, self-confident successful adults? How do you define success? Are your parenting tactics going to get them there? Does your parenting style build them up or tear them down?

When it comes to parenting, chances are you won't teach them everything they need to know to navigate adulthood. It kind of feels like all the rules keep changing, and the solutions that worked for your generation might be obsolete for your child's generation. However, if you teach them they are lovable and worth other people's time, and teach them how to ask for help from others, they'll be able to find the help they need to fill in the skills that you left blank.

You will make mistakes, but those mistakes don't have to be permanent. When you feel a decision you made in the past isn't working out the way you'd hoped, own up to it. Tell those you hurt that you are sorry. Explain why you made the choice you did. Tell them what you'd hoped the results would be, and propose a new course of action you think might work better. Take the first step to move in a better direction. You aren't perfect and neither are they. Do not forget to listen. Remember it is their life, they need to have a say in it. Mistakes can be learning experiences that draw you closer together, if you let them. The one thing a suicidal person needs most from you is your love. All the rest is just details that can be worked out along the way.

> *Love suffers long and is kind; love envies not; love flaunts not itself and is not puffed up, does not behave itself improperly, seeks not its own, is not easily provoked, thinks no evil; rejoices not in iniquity, but rejoices in the truth; bears all things, believes all things, hopes all things, and endures all things.*
> -1 Corinthians 13:4-7 MEV

> *So now abide faith, hope, and love, these three. But the greatest of these is love.*
> -1 Corinthians 13:13 MEV

This page is here for formatting purposes.

Chapter 26

Letting Go of Best Laid Plans

There is a saying that goes the best laid plans of mice and men often go awry, it originates from a poem called "To a Mouse" written by Robert Burns in 1785, but now days it is often used even by people who have never heard of the poem. It speaks of the futility of trying to plan for a future that you can't predict, and that is something that I think all of us can relate to. It does however beg the question: Why do the best laid plans of man go awry?

In 1961 Edward Lorenz decided to repeat some of the computations while running a numerical computer model to forecast the weather. While manually entering the initial conditions for the simulation Lorenz rounded the number at the third decimal point instead of at the sixth, and when he checked the results an hour later he was shocked by how different the weather was compared to the first simulation.

The small change had caused other small changes that increasingly compounded over time until they had affected basically everything. This is known as deterministic chaos or simply chaos and it means that the farther you want to predict into the future the more perfect your understanding of the present needs to be in order for your prediction to be accurate.

The New York Academy of Sciences published a paper by Edward Lorenz in February of 1963 in which Lorenz remarked on the implications of his findings saying:

> *"One meteorologist remarked that if the theory were correct, one flap of a sea gull's wings would be enough to alter the course of the weather forever. The controversy has not yet been settled, but the most recent evidence seems to favor the sea gulls."*
>
> — *Edward Lorenz, The Predictability of Hydrodynamic Flow*

Luckily this effect is not limited to merely the weather, or a power granted solely to sea gulls. Any change in the present no matter how small will affect the future and with time greatly change your circumstances. You don't need to fix everything in a day, or even have a long term plan on how to make everything better, sometimes a small step in the right direction is all you need to reap major rewards down the line.

If granted the choice, I think most people would prefer that things always go as planned, and nothing bad ever happened to them. Surely it stands to reason that the world where everyone is happy, and all your prayers are answered the moment you make them, must be the best possible world, but is it actually?

I doubt it. Difficulty encourages growth, and God knowing that, lets mankind face it for their benefit, but you don't have to face it alone. A burden shared is made lighter, God never intended for man to carry the weight of the world alone. That is why Jesus Himself promised us help:

> *"If you love Me, keep My commandments. I will pray the Father, and He will give you another Counselor, that He may be with you forever: the Spirit of truth, whom the world cannot receive, for it does not see Him, neither does it know Him. But you know Him, for He lives with you, and will be in you." — John 14:15-17 MEV*

Since chaos arises from an imperfect knowledge of the present and how the effects of the missing data will affect the future, in theory with complete understanding comes a complete lack of chaos. In philosophical discussions the theory that a super intelligent being with a complete knowledge of everything could predict the future with certainty was nick-named "Laplace's Demon" it goes like this:

> *We may regard the present state of the universe as the effect of its past and the cause of its future. An intellect which at a certain moment would know all forces that set nature in motion, and all positions of all items of which nature is composed, if this intellect were also vast enough to submit these data to analysis, it would embrace in a single formula the movements of the greatest bodies of the universe and those of the tiniest atom; for such an intellect nothing would be uncertain and the future just like the past would be present before its eyes.*
>
> *— Pierre Simon Laplace, A Philosophical Essay on Probabilities*

I find it fascinating that it is called Laplace's demon even though he himself did not use the word demon, merely an intelligence. Mankind often demonizes what we can't understand.

God is no demon, but He as the creator of everything, is an intelligence of the level described by Laplace. Better yet, nothing is stopping Him from making changes to bring about a better future than the one that would result if He did nothing, and since He has a perfect knowledge of the present, He can make plans on how best to do so, without chaos messing them up. He even says so Himself in the Book of Job:

Where were you when I laid the foundations of the earth? Declare, if you have understanding.
Who has determined its measurements, if you know? Or who has stretched the line upon it?
To what are its foundations fastened? Or who laid its cornerstone when the morning stars sang together, and all the sons of God shouted for joy?

Or who shut up the sea with doors when it broke forth and went out of the womb?
When I made the cloud its garment, and thick darkness its swaddling band, and broke up for it My decreed place, and set bars and doors, and said, 'This far you will come but no farther, and here your proud waves will be stopped'?

Have you commanded the morning in your days, and caused the dawn to know its place, that it might take hold of the ends of the earth, that the wicked might be shaken out of it?
It is turned like clay by the seal, and it stands out as a garment.
From the wicked their light is withheld, and the high arm will be broken.

Have you entered into the springs of the sea?
Or have you walked in search of the depths?
Have the gates of death been opened to you?
Or have you seen the doors of the shadow of death?
Have you perceived the breadth of the earth?
Declare, if you know it all.

— Job 38:4-18 MEV

In this passage God clearly makes a point that no man knows better than God, because He knows things that no one else could possibly know, but more than that He doesn't just simply know. He acts: Laid the foundation, determined its measurements, shut up the sea, commanded the morning, seen the doors of the shadow of death, these aren't just an awareness of circumstances, they are experiences. Things that God has done, and proof that He will not sit idly by leaving the world to its fate.

One Lenten season, (The forty days leading up to Easter), our Pastor asked us to surrender something to God. It could be a good work we intended to do more for that season, like help feed the poor, visit the sick, or pray more, or it could be a vice we were going to let go, like lying, cheating or swearing. Whatever we wanted to offer up to God, he wanted us to write it on a white flag with a black marker and put it in this sandbox located in the Commons area of the church.

I thought long and hard over what to write on that flag. Each week he encouraged us to participate, but I was in a really dark place that season. I didn't feel like I had anything good to offer. I felt like every area of my life deserved a big "Needs improvement" stamped all over it! Giving God something good was out of the question that year. I'd already taken inventory, and I had nothing good to offer. If I were going to give something to God, it was going to have to be a problem, because those were in no short supply! So which one did He want? Handing God one while holding back on the others felt like I'd be dropping every other ball, and I was exhausted from years of trying to juggle everything on my own.

Suddenly, I had my answer. I went to the display in the back of the church, and scribbled "I give everything to you." on my little white flag. I stabbed it into the sandbox and walked away. Unbeknownst to me, they took all those little white flags, and lined the church's driveway with our white flags on Good Friday.

When we drove to church that night we saw all our little white flags proudly waving as they lined the drive. After church, it rained like crazy that night! Holy Saturday, when the assistant pastor came to clean up all the little flags, he noticed mine said, "I give you everything" so he took a picture of it because it summed up all the flags in one. After all, everything is everything, right?

On Easter, they showed us a picture of my flag, but I noticed something different, and it brought me to tears. You see, only I knew that everything was problems, pain, darkness and grief. But with God's cleansing rain, He washed "Everything" away. Those dark words written in black ink had almost faded away in the picture before me. God showed me when I put my trust in Him, He can pick up the pieces of the mess I've made, and make a more beautiful work of art than I ever could have imagined before my struggles began.

It can feel like your prayers go unanswered sometimes, but that probably has more to due with God having a better plan than you know. Patience is sometimes required for the best results. Even if you were perfect in every way sometimes your suffering is for someone else's sake, even Jesus had to face intense suffering, but you can rest assured that all the suffering you endure will have an effect on the future and it will have been worth it.

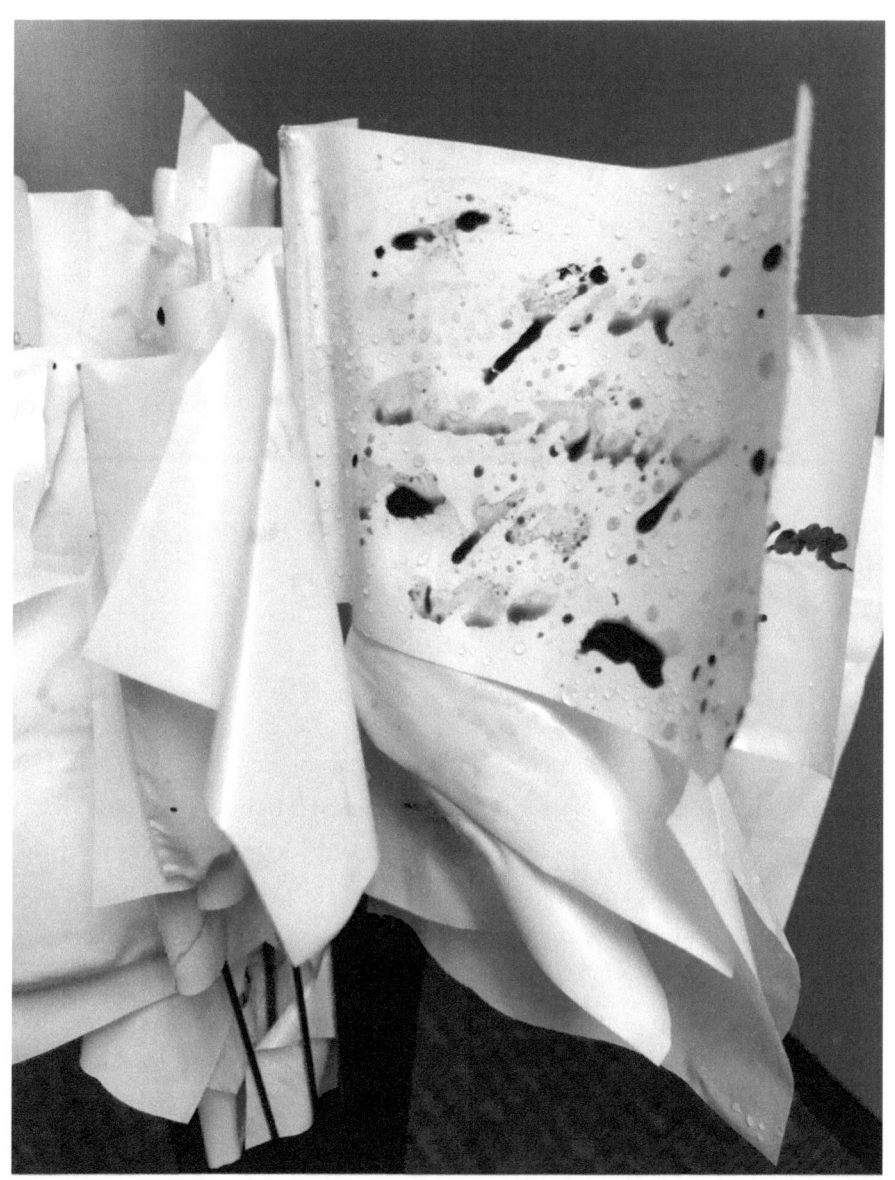

Chapter 27

Keep Going

During Joey's suicidal years it would have been safe to say all of us were miserable, but I can't really tell you what Michael's life was like. I was too exhausted trying to handle mine and Joey's problems to think to even ask. He never really talked about it, but Michael probably was struggling as much as we were, and just didn't say anything. Remember, he's the one who tried to drown himself without any warning to the rest of us. The fact of the matter is some suicidal kids warn you and others do not! You have to watch out for everyone you love because everyone needs to know that they matter to someone. Otherwise, they might just give up. Don't just assume your loved ones are handling their life well. Ask them how things are going and if there's anything you can do to help.

People have suicidal thoughts because they find their life unbearable. If you want to help them choose to live, you have to help them carve out a life for themselves that rewards, inspires and motivates them. There's a saying, "You can lead a horse to water, but you can't make it drink." They will have to make their own life choices. You have to give them the love and support to convince them they are capable of doing so.

When it comes right down to it, we can't force anyone to live. The decision to complete a suicide is between them and God. You can't be there every moment of every day. You have to sleep sometime, and even if you could be there every moment, the mere act of watching their every move would probably be more creepy than helpful.

What you can do is model Christ's love for them. Accept them for who they are. Make them feel welcome, needed, and loved. Pray for them often, and accept that God loves them more than you are capable of loving them, and He loved them before you ever knew them. Trust God's plan for them and let Him take care of their needs when you can't. A good motto to follow would be the Serenity Prayer that has been used by Alcoholic's Anonymous for years. It goes as follows:

> *"God grant me the serenity to accept the things I can not change,*
>
> *The Courage to change the things I can,*
>
> *And the wisdom to know the difference."*
>
> —*Reinhold Niebuhr*

I asked Joey once what he thought got him through his High School years as he ping-ponged between a rock and a hard place, and he said it was three simple things. Here's what he told me in his own words:

"One, my brother was always willing to listen to my B. S.

Two, you were always willing to love me, in spite of my B. S.

And three, God had a plan for my life, and I just have to wait and see what it is."

Months later, Joey saw me still struggling to get the book written. He said, "What's the hold up? I thought your book was about how to help a suicidal person you care about. I already gave you the answer. So what is taking so long?"

I said, "I'm not sure I've learned the lesson enough to teach it to anyone else. Honestly, some days I feel like I'm still in the lake treading water."

"Of course you are." Joey replied "We all are. That lake is called life and you won't get out of that lake until you die. The best you can do is keep swimming and encourage everyone you meet to keep swimming too."

I wish I was half as brilliant as him! God has a perfect plan for each of us, and our hearts won't rest until they rest in Him. Life is a struggle, but the struggle will be worth it in the end. So for now, spend time with your kids. Let them know that they are loved, and you are proud of them. Bathe them in prayer. Keep swimming, and teach them to swim too.

God bless you always.

Special Thanks

Since it took me over ten years to complete this book, I must say I am so grateful for everyone who encouraged me along on my journey. First of all, God for providing the miracles that gave me a reason for writing. Don, my children, step-children and grand-kids, who love me and forgive me, as I figure this thing called life out. As I blunder along they love me in spite of my mistakes. Thank you so much! You'll never know how very very much I love you all.

All of my extended family, that loved and support us through this, and all the other minor set backs of life. Life is so much easier when you have a strong family to lean on! Thanks to you, I never had to spend a single night on the streets, even though I was technically homeless twice. Daddy always said, "Blood is thicker than water." and Mama said, "The family that prays together stays together." You proved both their points. Thank you.

My dear friends Lorna Worley and Aunt Joyce C, who listened every time I talked about this project and encouraged me each step of the way. You insisted I could do this, every time I felt like giving up.

Betsy, Clark and Dennis Conant, and James Haldane who reviewed an early copy of my entire manuscript and checked it both for accuracy and readability. I appreciate your encouragement and trust your opinions. Thanks to you, I have the courage to put this out there for the world to read.

Most especially, you the reader, for trusting me enough to invite me into your life, to share with you our story. I pray that knowing the mistakes we made will help you make less of your own.

About The Author:

Born the eleventh of twelve kids, Cyndi C. now has three children and four grown step-kids who have children and grand-children of their own. Having experienced the success of being a business owner, and later plummeted to homeless single-mother status, Cyndi has lead an eventful life, but thanks to the love and support of her wonderful family, and God's protective Grace, it has been an adventure full of laughter even in the darkest times. Cyndi now lives in her country home with her husband, Don, her three boys, two dogs and two cats.

www.ingramcontent.com/pod-product-compliance
Lightning Source LLC
Chambersburg PA
CBHW020909080526
44589CB00011B/515